IMAGES
of America

LAWRENCE
MASSACHUSETTS

To raise funds for the German Red Cross during World War I, Cora Trumpold (left) and Gretchen Beilig (right), both of Lawrence, created a living tableau of Miss Liberty and Miss Germany. The bell was rung each time they received a contribution. Adolph St. Linger, a designer for the Everett Mill, took this photograph in 1916.

IMAGES
of America

LAWRENCE
MASSACHUSETTS

Eartha Dengler, Katherine Khalife,
and Ken Skulski

ARCADIA
PUBLISHING

Copyright © 1995 by Immigrant City Archives
ISBN 978-1-5316-6090-1

Published by Arcadia Publishing
Charleston, South Carolina

For all general information contact Arcadia Publishing at:
Telephone 843-853-2070
Fax 843-853-0044
E-mail sales@arcadiapublishing.com
For customer service and orders:
Toll-Free 1-888-313-2665

Visit us on the Internet at www.arcadiapublishing.com

Lawrence's famous Theater Row on Broadway, as it appeared one night in 1940.

FRONT COVER ILLUSTRATION: Sebastiano and Rosaria Catalano married in Italy in 1920 before sailing for America, arriving only two days before this photograph was taken. Posed in front of a fruit store owned by their relatives at 8 1/2 Osgood Street, the Catalanos looked forward to establishing themselves as new Lawrencians. Two years later they became the proud owners of their own grocery store at 77 Newbury Street. From left to right are: (front row) Irene DiPaola, Maria DiPaola, and Rosaria Catalano; (back row) Sebatiano Catalano and Sebastiano DiPaola.

Contents

Introduction   7

1.   The Essex Company   9

2.   We Weave the World's Worsteds   25

3.   The City Grows Up   43

4.   Body, Mind, and Spirit   59

5.   Essex Street   75

6.   Memorable Events   89

7.   A Sense of Neighborhood   99

8.   All Work, No Play?   117

Acknowledgments   128

Design for a City Seal,
adopted by concurrent
vote of the City Council
Augᵗ 22ᵈ 1853

G. W. Benson
City Clerk

Introduction

Lawrence, Massachusetts, the Immigrant City, earned its nickname more than 100 years ago when, as home to 54 different nationalities, 80% of its population was either foreign born or first-generation American. The causes and ramifications of this remarkable mixture made Lawrence a microcosm of American society at large. As such, its story is one that deserves to be told, not only in the local area but also beyond.

Uniquely separated in time and space from its more affluent neighbors, Lawrence began in 1845 as a planned textile town organized, developed, and managed by a corporation of Yankee investors called the Essex Company. Rising from former farmlands along the banks of the Merrimack River, this well-planned and quickly growing industrial community became a thriving city in less than ten years.

Sitting as it did in a rural landscape, Lawrence truly brought "the machine into the garden." This contradiction between the republican ideal of a small town atmosphere and the beehive activity of a manufacturing city was one the Essex Company intended to reconcile by planning and building its model town. The men in charge had visions and dreams of a new textile city that would exist both to provide profits to investors *and* to benefit the common citizens living and working within its boundaries. The "New City on the Merrimack" was indeed going to be a great experiment.

Although New England migrants—considered by Lawrence's founders to be the stable base of citizenry—flocked to the new community to work as tradesmen, mill hands, and shopkeepers, the large demand for manpower meant that "foreigners" would also be needed to turn the dream of a great new textile center into a reality. Thus immigrant labor flooded into Lawrence, at first to work on construction of the dam, canals, factories, and boarding houses, and later to work in the mills. Because the need for large numbers of immigrant workers conflicted with the desire to keep the town under the control of Yankee natives, foreigners were only slowly accepted as part of the permanent population.

For many of them, Lawrence was the first stop after arriving in the United States. And for most, it was at first a place of hardship, loneliness, low-paying jobs, and discrimination. Here they learned the language and customs of their new country and acquired the skills needed to compete in the labor market—a strange place for people coming from rural origins in faraway lands!

The men of the Essex Company were aware of the need to integrate immigrants and promote their assimilation in order to avoid conflicts at work sites and in the neighborhoods. They decided that public education would be the most effective way through which foreigners could be brought into the folds of established society.

The Lawrence school system was organized with the help of education reformer Horace Mann. Beginning in the 1850s, the city gathered all the elements necessary to educate its varied citizenry: young and old, native and non-English speaking, workers needing evening schools and students wanting to upgrade technical skills. In addition, churches started parochial schools, immigrant societies encouraged their members to learn English, and several free libraries were organized by textile mills.

For many factory workers, and especially immigrants, education was not enough to insure job security and advancement. It was necessary to belong to a security system of fraternal or mutual aid societies organized to provide help in case of death, illness, or unemployment. These clubs were usually formed by men, while women most often relied on friends, co-workers, and sympathetic neighbors for assistance.

In 1905 Robert H. Tewksbury, treasurer of the Essex Company for thirty-seven years and the most important historian of the city, wrote: "Sociologists view with great interest the experiment of bringing together here, in one industrial community, representatives of every civilized race and are surprised to find all dwelling in amity, controlled only by the prompting patriotism, all alike seeking the rewards of toil. Such an exhibition of the brotherhood of man they see in Lawrence."

The planned city nevertheless experienced numerous pressures as its textile industry expanded. More available work and falling passenger fares on ships from overseas soon caused an increase in the number of immigrants, with a resulting deterioration of living space and a lowering of wages. Conditions in Lawrence reflected many national trends—felt here with greater intensity because of the city's small area and the incredible number of nationalities living in its crowded tenement districts.

All the traditional adversaries—skilled and unskilled labor, immigrant and old-timer, men and women—united in the Great Strike of 1912 to rebel against a common enemy: mill owners and management. Language differences were overcome through the help of strike leaders and, for almost three months, people organized, walked the picket lines, and helped each other to win the strike. To the amazement of the mill hierarchy, the solidarity of even the most needy strikers could not be broken by promises of work. Exploitation of the traditional differences between nationalities, and of the long-standing rivalries between unskilled workers and trade unions, suddenly became impossible.

After World War II Lawrence's woolen and worsted industry was confronted by new problems: obsolete buildings, machinery unsuitable for the production of artificial fibers, and increasing pressure from labor unions to pay better wages and guarantee job security. The southern states offered many appealing advantages, and by the 1950s almost all the textile mills had left Lawrence. Twenty thousand jobs had been lost.

New industries came in to fill some of the gaps, but were never able to provide the entry level positions which had once given new immigrants a place in the workforce with a chance to move up. Once again, Lawrence was the barometer of national trends to come. The collapse of the textile industry here foreshadowed the problems soon to be encountered by other major U.S. industries.

Today Lawrence is a city of 70,000, not very different from many other industrial communities that have seen better days. Almost half of the city's population is now of Hispanic origin, either from Puerto Rico or the Caribbean countries. Unlike some other cities, however, Lawrence still has the ability to renew itself, its neighborhoods, and its main streets because of the constant inflow of energetic young newcomers.

The history of Lawrence deserves to be told, not just because of the lives of its famous people, the tales of its labor struggles, or the immensity of its giant brick mills, but because the city has always been home to new immigrants and their offspring who move out into American society from here. Lawrence, on less than 7 square miles, continues to carry the special responsibilities of preparing newcomers to become Americans.

Immigrant City Archives was established in 1978 to collect and preserve the history of Lawrence and its people. The organization's name underscores its unique mission: to focus on the diversity of the population, the process of assimilation, and the acceptance of the newcomer by the old-timer—which, in Lawrence, has often meant the immigrant of the previous decade.

The Archives has collected thousands of historical photographs—the most popular medium through which immigrants recorded life in the neighborhood, family, and at work. In addition, there are many manuscripts, oral and video biographies, and printed materials documenting individuals, organizations, and businesses.

Although a number of books, articles, dissertations, films, and exhibits have made use of research and material from Immigrant City Archives, this book is the first to consist *entirely* of photographs and images from its collection.

8

One

The Essex Company

South-western View of Lawrence.

Lawrence was planned as a model textile town by its founding corporation, the Essex Company. Beginning in 1845 with the construction of the Great Stone Dam, the firm laid out the city, engineered and built mills and public works projects, contributed sites for parks and churches, sold land, and leased waterpower.

By the time this engraving of the Upper Pacific, Atlantic, and Washington Mills was made in 1861, Lawrence had evolved from plans on paper into a thriving community with a population of more than 18,400. The city was on its way.

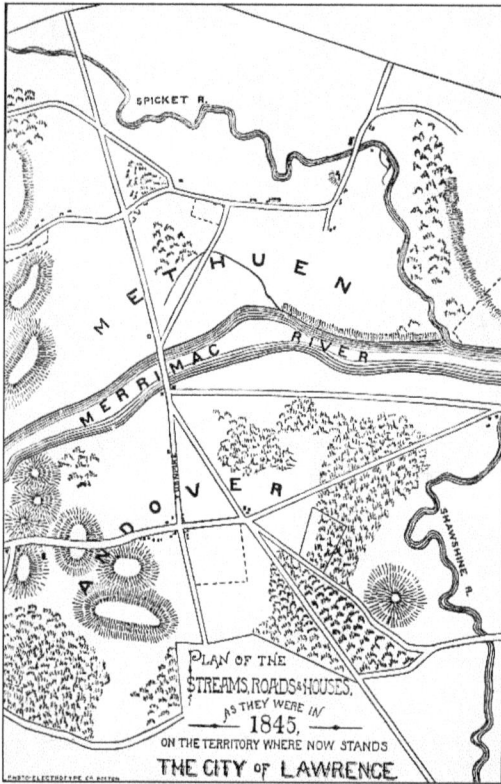

PLAN OF THE STREAMS, ROADS & HOUSES, AS THEY WERE IN 1845, ON THE TERRITORY WHERE NOW STANDS THE CITY OF LAWRENCE

Lawrence occupies territory that was originally part of Andover and Methuen. The city's 7 square miles were assembled from parcels purchased from landowners on both sides of the Merrimack River surrounding Bodwell's Falls, the planned site of the Great Stone Dam. There was only one bridge crossing the river in Lawrence in 1845. Called Andover Bridge, it had been built as a toll bridge near Bodwell's Falls in 1793. Upon its completion it became the area's main river crossing, replacing Marston's ferry, located at the foot of Ferry Street, and Bodwell's ferry, located near the old pumping station.

Taken from atop the Upper Pacific Mills chimney about 1870, this photograph shows the Boston and Maine Railroad Bridge (left) and Andover Bridge (right, closest to the dam). During Lawrence's early construction days, this was the busiest spot in town. Tolls were collected on Andover Bridge until 1868 and the structure remained in use until 1881.

The earliest vision of a "New City on the Merrimack," as Lawrence was often called prior to incorporation, was in the mind and eye of Daniel Saunders, an Andover woolen manufacturer. Having observed the success of Lowell's mills, Saunders determined the waterpower potential of the Merrimack at Bodwell's Falls to be just as great.

In 1843, along with Samuel Lawrence and others, Saunders established the Merrimack Water Power Association, the precursor of the Essex Company. As agent of the group, it was Saunders' job to secure the purchase of necessary land on both sides of the river.

The Saunders family lived in this brick house from 1842 to 1884. It stood on the southwest corner of what is now South Broadway and Andover Street until being razed in 1950. Daniel Saunders—whose sons Daniel Jr. and Caleb both served as mayors of Lawrence—lived here until his death in 1872. Saunders was a local leader in the anti-slavery movement and reportedly used his home as a station on the Underground Railroad, helping to hide escaped slaves before the Civil War.

Few individuals have left a more enduring imprint on Lawrence than Charles S. Storrow. Born in Montreal in 1809, he graduated from Harvard and studied further with prominent civil engineer Loammi Baldwin. Encouraged by family friend General Lafayette, Storrow decided to continue his education in France, then in England, before returning to Boston in 1832. Shortly thereafter he assisted in the construction of New England's first passenger railroad, the Boston and Lowell, and became its manager and agent for nearly ten years.

When the Essex Company formed in 1845, Storrow was named director, treasurer, agent, and chief engineer. He served as the first mayor of Lawrence when the town became a city in 1853. The Storrow School was named in his honor.

As chief engineer of the Essex Company, Storrow designed many of Lawrence's public works projects, early mill buildings, churches, and schools. As town planner he laid out streets and parks that were the envy of other communities for years to come.

One of his greatest achievements, however, was the Great Stone Dam, a 1,629-foot-long engineering wonder built from granite blocks set in hydraulic cement. For several years it was the longest dam in the world. Since its completion in 1848, it has served the city without fail.

A view from the Great Stone Dam looking northeasterly, *c.* 1886. The mills in the background were part of the Pacific Mills Corporation; the iron bridge—located approximately where Andover Bridge once stood—was replaced by the current Falls Bridge in 1935. At right, where the man stands with his net, is the fishway that helped migrating schools navigate the dam. Fish were plentiful. At one time, commercial fishing took place from wharves along the river's north bank and fishing rights were valuable commodities to those who earned their livings catching "Merrimack beef."

In this winter photograph of the dam taken in the 1870s, a seemingly untouched Tower Hill lies to the left in the background. To its right, near Water Street, is a small bridge leading to a lumber dock. Farther to the right, the large building with the "smokeless" smokestack may have belonged to the Pacific Brewery, once located in the Essex Yard (see p. 53). At far right is the Pacific House, a popular nineteenth-century hotel.

13

Designed by Charles S. Storrow, the North Canal was constructed from 1845 to 1848. Running parallel to the Merrimack, it created an artificial island crowded with textile mills. This photograph, taken c. 1900 looking west, shows portions of the Atlantic and Pacific Mills to the left, with Canal Street on the right. The Moseley Truss Bridge, seen here spanning the canal, can be found today on the grounds of Merrimack College, where it has been restored.

The North Canal is just over a mile long. At its origin it is 100 feet wide, narrowing to 60 feet at the wasteway where it joins the Spicket River and flows back into the Merrimack. The waste weir, shown here in 1875, is located off Canal Street just below Marston Street.

The North Canal's lower locks and lock-keeper's house as they appeared in 1897. Since waterpower for the mills was dependent on sufficient water levels in the canal, extended droughts often caused factory closings during dry summers. When steam power and then electricity came along, the problem was eliminated.

An interior view of the North Canal gatehouse, 1898. Tom Holmes, a gate tender for the Essex Company, operates the head gates' hoisting apparatus, allowing water from the Merrimack to enter the canal.

Abbott Lawrence, born in Groton, Massachusetts, in 1792, was the largest investor in the city that now bears his name. A businessman, politician, diplomat, and philanthropist, Lawrence almost became vice president of the United States in 1848.

He was the first president and one of the original directors of the Essex Company, along with Nathan Appleton, Ignatius Sargent, Patrick T. Jackson, John A. Lowell, William Sturgis, and Charles S. Storrow. He also served as president of both the Atlantic and Pacific Mills before his death in 1855.

The city's oldest industrial landmark is the Lawrence Machine Shop, shown here from the front and back. Originally constructed for the Essex Company from 1846 to 1848, the "old stone mill" eventually turned out steam locomotives, water wheels, trip hammers, pumps, stationary engines, lathes, textile machinery, and printing presses. A passenger engine named "Abbott Lawrence" was manufactured here in 1852 for the Rochester and Syracuse Railroad. Although the Machine Shop ceased operations in 1857, its buildings were purchased by the Everett Mills and still remain in use today.

The first offices of the Essex Company were housed in a frame building which was later moved to the dam to serve as the gatekeeper's house. In 1846 Charles Bigelow constructed this new granite office building for the firm. It was located in front of the Machine Shop at the foot of Essex Street, now the site of the Everett Mills.

George Sanborn, for whom Sanborn Street was named, was one of the earliest arrivals to the Essex Company's "New City on the Merrimack." So new was it that when he first moved here from Epping, N.H., in July 1845 to work as a carpenter for the company, he couldn't find a room to rent or a bed on which to sleep. Sanborn stayed on, though, working for the Essex Company for fifty-two years. He is pictured here in 1881, seated in a wagon in front of the company's carpenter shop on Methuen Street.

Hiram F. Mills, a Maine native and 1856 graduate of Rensselaer Polytechnic Institute, apprenticed with Charles S. Storrow. In 1869 he was named chief engineer of the Essex Company, where he devised experiments leading to significant improvements in American methods of water measurement.

In the 1880s Mills established the Lawrence Experiment Station on Island Street. Devoted entirely to experiments in water purification and sewage disposal, it was the first center of its kind in the nation. Within a short time Mills was recognized as the father of a new specialty—sanitary engineering. He made many other contributions to public health as well, including the design of the filter beds on Water Street.

In the 1880s Mills designed and constructed the Essex Company compound at 6 Essex Street, at the corner of Union. This building, one of five structures in the complex, housed the company's headquarters until December 1989. Four years later the compound became home to Immigrant City Archives, the historical society of Lawrence and its people.

An interior view of the Essex Company's second floor office in 1898. From left to right are Walter Spear, Richard A. Hale, J. Harry Anderson, Fred Palmer, Clarence H. Rooks, Daniel A. Danahy, and John D. Dickie.

Robert H. Tewksbury, shown here in his office about 1890, worked for the Essex Company for many years as a cashier and land agent. He became mayor of Lawrence in 1875 and was also a well-respected historian, writer, and businessman. At the time of his death in 1910, he resided at 20 Berkeley Street. Tewksbury Street in South Lawrence is named for him.

SMALL MILL LOTS

—AND—

WATER POWER,

For Mechanical and Manufacturing Purposes, in the

CITY OF LAWRENCE, MASS.

TO BE SOLD BY THE ESSEX COMPANY AT AUCTION,

July 15, 1858, at 4 o'clock P. M., on the premises.

TWELVE LOTS

Lying on the main Canal at Lawrence, opposite the LAWRENCE MACHINE SHOP, and just below the PEMBERTON and LAWRENCE DUCK COMPANIES, containing from 28,000 to 31,500 square feet each. Appurtenant to each lot one third of a

"MILL POWER"

equivalent to more than 20 horse power; subject to a water rent of $300 a year, payable semi-annually. No rent to be charged until after March 1, 1860, but the power may be brought into use immediately. Additional Power, if wanted, may be had at the same rate.

Every Lot will be Offered and Sold Without Reserve,

to the highest bidder. TERMS—one quarter Cash, and three quarters in three equal notes, payable in one, two, and three years respectively, with interest annually, secured by mortgage, or one quarter cash and three quarters in stock of the Company at par, at the option of purchasers. The deed of conveyance will be an Indenture of two parts, similar to those conveying land and water power to the Paper Mills, Grist Mills, &c., at the lower end of the Canal. The power is as permanent and is guarantied to the purchasers as fully as that furnished to any of the large manufacturing corporations in Lawrence.

CHARLES S. STORROW, Treasurer of Essex Company.

N. A. THOMPSON & CO., Auct'rs.

One of the Essex Company's major activities was selling land for housing, business, and industry. On a number of occasions public auctions were held. The first one, in April 1846, drew crowds to bid on lots with boundaries marked off by furrows in the dirt. Parcels on Haverhill Street and on Essex Street brought anywhere from 9 to 70¢ per square foot that day.

In the earliest days of the "new city," worshipers had no church buildings to attend. Seeing the need, the Essex Company donated lots to groups who, until then, had been meeting anywhere they could find room. In 1846 Grace Episcopal became the first church to be erected. Abbott, Samuel, and Amos Lawrence were among the early financial contributors. The present stone church, located on the same site, was built in 1851 and enlarged in 1896.

Once located near the corner of Chestnut and White Streets, Immaculate Conception was the first Roman Catholic church in Lawrence, established by Reverend Charles Ffrench in 1846. Although this photograph does not show the original wooden structure, it does provide a glimpse of the rectory and, at the far right, a portion of the Protectory of Mary Immaculate.

Initially, Father Ffrench ministered to the Irish who, in the 1840s, constituted the largest group of Catholics here. Legend has it that during the summer of 1845, he offered the first Mass in Lawrence in a Water Street sawmill, and the second in a shanty across the river in South Lawrence. After his death in 1851, he was succeeded by Reverend James Taaffe, founder of the Protectory and the Catholic Friends' Society.

The Essex Company wasted no time in bringing its development plans to fruition. Lawrence became an official Massachusetts town in 1847 and received its city charter six years later. This c. 1854 view, looking from Prospect Hill, gives a clear sense of how carefully the city's layout was planned—and how much actual building had taken place in the first nine years. By the time this lithograph was created, Lawrence had fourteen churches, fourteen public schools, fifteen

manufacturing companies, and a population of 15,000. The buildings are, clockwise from the left foreground: the Lawrence Machine Shop, Duck Mills, Pemberton Mills, Bay State Mills, Atlantic Mills, and Upper Pacific Mills. City Hall is in the center of the photograph, and the rectangular structure to the right is Mechanics' Block, built by the Essex Company in 1847 as housing for Machine Shop employees.

The construction of the South Canal head works, near the Great Stone Dam, around 1865. South Canal construction began in the 1860s and was originally intended to reach as far as South Union Street. The first portion was built from just above the dam to Parker Street. This part of the canal was 60 feet wide and 10 feet deep, providing waterpower to the diverse group of industries lining its banks. An extension was made in 1896 and pipes were later laid to reach the Wood and Ayer Mills when they were erected.

A view of the South Canal head gates and gatehouse, at about the time of the canal's completion. This photograph was taken from a bridge crossing the canal at South Broadway, near Wolcott Avenue; a more modern version crosses at the same location today. In the background are homes on Shattuck Street.

Two

We Weave the World's Worsteds

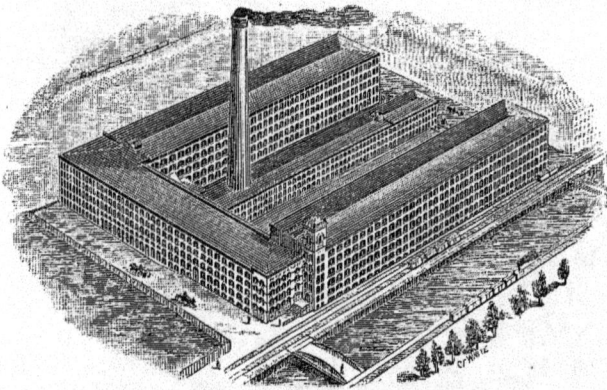

SPINNERS OF WORSTED YARNS.

OF ALL

QUALITIES AND NUMBERS

FOR

WORSTED COATINGS,
DRESS GOODS and
KNIT WEAR,

Yarns Spun on both the Bradford and French Systems.

SPECIALTY:
UNIFORMITY OF COLOR.

Also Woolen and Merino Yarns, and Coarse Yarns for Backing.

WASHINGTON MILLS COMPANY, LAWRENCE, MASS.

Although some of the textile mills in Lawrence manufactured cotton fabrics, it was the staggering amount of woolens produced here that made the city famous. By the 1890s, worsted yarns and goods became the dominant part of Lawrence's woolen industry. Producing a very durable cloth for suits and coats, worsted yarn was made from sheep's wool selected for its length and smooth but hard surface, spun into yarn with a tight twist.

With worsted's growth in popularity and the building of the huge Wood and Ayer Mills in the early 1900s, it wasn't long until Lawrence became the woolen and worsted center of the world. Even children were proud of that distinction; "We Weave the World's Worsteds" became a familiar phrase in schools around the city.

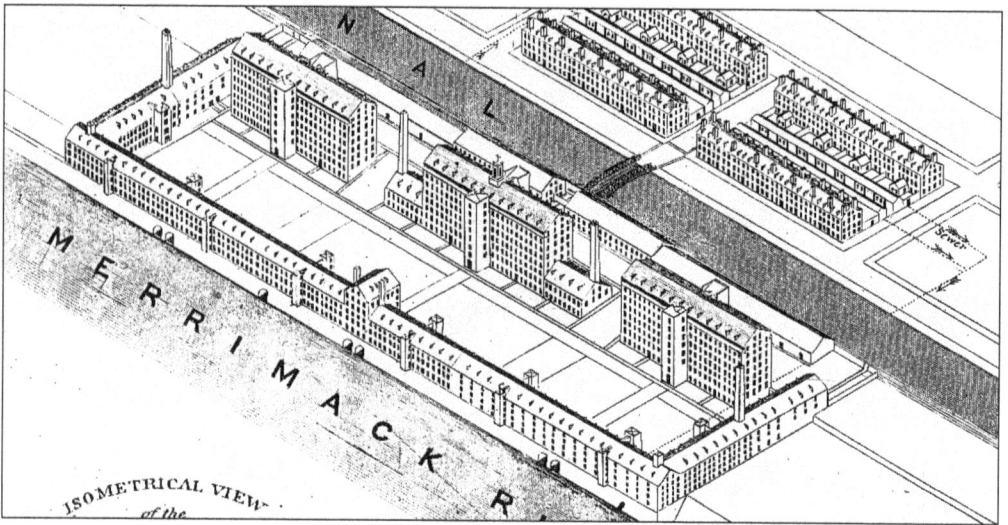

ISOMETRICAL VIEW
of the

The earliest textile mill established in Lawrence was the Bay State, which began construction in 1846. It soon became world famous for its woolen dress fabrics, especially the plaid "Bay State Shawl" exhibited in 1852 at the first International Exposition. During the depression of 1857 the company failed and was eventually replaced by the Washington Mills.

The boarding houses visible in this 1850 graphic were located just across the North Canal on Canal and Methuen Streets, between Jackson and Newbury. They were built at the same time as the mills to accommodate operatives. The Visitors Center of the Lawrence Heritage State Park now occupies the only section still standing.

Bell Time, a graphic by Winslow Homer, was published in Harper's Weekly in July 1868. The Washington Mills provide the backdrop for textile workers with lunch pails in hand. Men and women, young and old, were called to work from boarding houses and tenements by factory bells. Bells in churches, schools, and mills ruled the workers' day because clocks and watches were a luxury.

Henry K. Oliver, known as General Oliver, was one of the most extraordinary individuals in the early history of Lawrence. He resigned as Adjutant General of Massachusetts to become the first agent of the Atlantic Cotton Mills in 1848.

An effective mill manager, Oliver cared for his employees and was concerned for their well being. He established a free library and bathing facilities for workers and offered free lectures and concerts to Lawrencians. Oliver was elected to the school committee in 1853 and became mayor in 1858. He was a great benefactor to Lawrence's schools and working people.

The buildings of the Atlantic Mills, shown here c. 1905, occupied the central site on the mill island created by the Merrimack and the North Canal. Construction started in June 1846, and the mill began operating two years later. In 1913 ownership was transferred to the Pacific Mills. Most of the original Atlantic was demolished within the next few years, made necessary by the construction of the Central Bridge.

An early stereo view of corporation boarding houses on Canal Street, looking west from Amesbury to Hampshire. Originally built by 1848 for workers of the Atlantic Mills, they were operated by the corporation as a not-for-profit accommodation. Most mill girls took advantage of this housing until mixed housing, operated by independent boarding house keepers, was accepted in the 1860s.

With Canal Street boarding houses in the background, new turbines destined for the Lower Pacific Mills are being inspected at the North Canal around 1919. Ongoing improvements in the design of turbines frequently resulted in new sets being installed to replace outdated equipment. In many Lawrence mills the turbines are still present, but very few produce power today.

Maria Tomacchio, an Italian immigrant girl, was fifteen years old when this photograph was taken in the spinning room of the Ayer Mill, *c*. 1918. She looked confident and ready to make a good life for herself in America and, in the beginning, living as a boarder with Italian families made the transition easy.

For many women, however, that would all change after marriage, as the double burden of mill work and homemaking made for a hard life and few rewards. The ability of women to make friends and become part of a network of co-workers, neighbors, and family was important for survival in immigrant communities.

Of all the early textile mills in Lawrence, the Pacific—seen here in 1890—was the grandest both in size and importance. Commencing operations in 1853, it rapidly grew to employ thousands, becoming one of the largest manufacturers of cotton, worsted, and woolen goods in the world.

The company established both a library and relief society for employees and, at the Paris Exposition in 1867, received recognition from the Emperor Napoleon III for its efforts in advancing the material, intellectual, and moral welfare of its workers.

These Pacific Mills weavers were photographed in 1914, as World War I, which would eventually involve the U.S., began in Europe. Since many mill workers were European immigrants with family ties overseas, there was deep concern for the welfare of loved ones. In general, peace was kept between nationalities at work and in neighborhoods.

Wool sorting was a skilled job and many English immigrants were employed for this process. Wool had to be sorted for length, thickness, curl, and softness, and only an experienced pair of hands could feel the difference upon touch.

In 1910, when the average textile worker's pay was $5 to $8 per week, wool sorters made about $15. Although wool sorting was a desirable job and one into which it was difficult to advance, it was also dangerous; raw wool could transmit the deadly anthrax bacillus, leading to pulmonary failure.

The Pacific Mills Marching Band, typical of bands supported by many Lawrence textile mills, competed for attention at the parades and concerts which were popular weekend entertainment in the city. Groups such as the Arlington Mills Band gained notice beyond just Lawrence, becoming well known throughout Essex County for their talent and style. Since bands were maintained even during lay-off times, being part of one not only offered prestige but a form of job security as well.

The Lower Pacific Mills were not built until 1863, on a site which had originally been reserved for the Atlantic Mills. Worsted manufacturing took place in the Lower Pacific and some of the earliest power jacquard looms in the industry were also installed here. Two stories were later added to the mill and the twin towers were removed.

The new Pacific Print Works on Merrimack Street was completed in 1911, when operations formerly done in Dover, N.H., were consolidated with those done in Lawrence. While textile printing was the works' main concern, dyeing and bleaching of cotton fabrics also took place here, with many children working near hazardous chemicals. The Print Works, owned by the Pacific Mills Corporation, ceased operations in the 1950s and today serves as a business complex called Riverwalk.

The above photograph is of the Print Works Color Shop office staff in 1914. Mr. Kenyon is seated; standing, from left to right, are Mr. Farnworth, Mr. Hefte, and Mr. Whelpley.

The photograph below, taken in the same year, is of the Printing Room. This is where cotton goods received their patterns, also designed at the Pacific Mills.

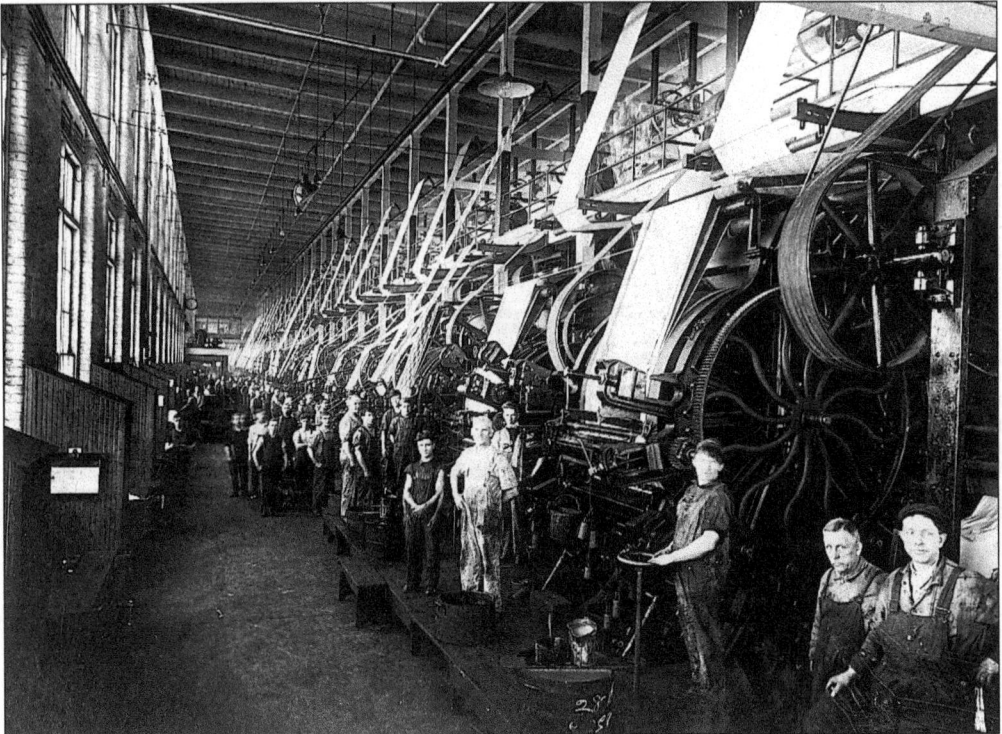

The Arlington Mills Corporation actually began here in a former piano case factory owned and operated by Abiel Stevens near the Spicket River. The Arlington took over his factory in 1865, making modifications, but it wasn't long until the buildings burned to the ground. A replacement was constructed in 1867 and remained until being demolished in 1888—this time to make room for massive new structures which would form the enormous Arlington Mills complex seen above.

Although it became one of the largest and best known woolen and worsted mills in the world, Arlington produced a wide variety of cotton goods as well.

Prior to World War I, the William Whitman Company, owner of other textile mills in Massachusetts and South Carolina, took over operation of the Arlington and continued building additions. The Katama, Acadia, and Monomac Mills were also once under the control of this important Lawrence employer.

ARLINGTON MILLS

NEWS *and* VIEWS

VOL. II   No. 5   LAWRENCE, MASSACHUSETTS   SEPTEMBER, 1942

Arlington Mills News and Views was one of several in-house publications produced by Lawrence textile mills to report on people and events in their factories. During World Wars I and II, stories of employees serving in the U.S. Armed Forces were also included.

The image on this 1942 cover illustrates how many women joined the work force to replace men gone off to war. When veterans returned to claim their spots on the machines, however, a lot of these women were forced out of mill jobs and back into more traditional roles.

35

This panoramic view of the Arlington Mills Girls Marching Group was taken following a parade on July 4, 1923. Notice the handmade costumes and the unique cloth "shield" carried by the leader. Factory employees from around the area were frequent participants in city parades, often even constructing their own floats.

Mill girls were usually friends from the same neighborhood, sharing the same ethnic background. The factories where they spent so many hours were an extension of their social circle and it was in the interest of mill management to support this team spirit. Sports, bands, and marching groups were popular expressions of competition among the mills of Lawrence.

American Woolen Co., Washington Mills.
Lawrence, Mass.

The Washington Mills, located on the mill island, replaced the earlier buildings of the Bay State Mills. Until 1890 the Washington was the largest woolen factory in the United States. By 1899 its production had shifted to worsted goods and ownership had been assumed by the American Woolen Company. The buildings, left vacant in the 1950s when the textile industry left Lawrence and moved south, are now home to various types of small industries.

Carpenters in the Washington Mills Carpenter Shop were members of the Carpenter and Joiners Union, organized in the nineteenth century. The shop's tools are proudly displayed in the foreground of this c. 1901 photograph.

Seen here from atop the Washington Mills chimney in 1886 is the original Duck Bridge, connecting Union Street with South Union. Built in the 1850s, it burned down a year after this photograph was taken. Replaced by a metal structure in 1888, the bridge takes its name from the Lawrence Duck Company, incorporated in 1853. The Duck Mills, which stood on the corner of Union and Canal Streets, produced a cotton cloth called duck, used to make sails and a variety of other canvas products. Only a portion of the original mills remains today.

The vacant land to the right of the river in this photograph is a South Lawrence site used for circuses and other activities. In 1906 the giant Wood Mill was built here.

Child labor was always employed by the textile industry and only gradually was legislation passed to establish adequate standards. It took until 1938 for effective regulations to be in place nationwide.

Just a few years before this c. 1916 group photograph of young Washington Mill workers was taken, another child employed at the same mill was scalped. Camella Teoli was hospitalized for seven months after the injury, incurred when her hair became tangled in machinery.

Born of Portuguese immigrants who settled on Martha's Vineyard, William Wood was among the most influential, dynamic, and wealthy mill men of all time. Beginning as a mill hand in New Bedford and Fall River, Wood moved up the corporate ladder rather quickly, eventually marrying the daughter of Frederick Ayer, a millionaire patent medicine manufacturer whose company headquarters was in Lowell.

Together, these two men established the vast American Woolen Company, which at one time had sixty mills in seven states, producing a total of more than eighty million yards of woolen and worsted cloth each year.

Wood, who built his baronial estate in Andover, spent most of his adult life mired in controversy. He committed suicide in 1926.

Of all the mills owned by the American Woolen Company, the Wood Mill, built in 1906, was the crown jewel. The largest worsted mill in the world, the main building had two wings, each a half-mile long, connected by the office section on South Union Street. Constructed by nine hundred men in just eight months, the mill could process as much as a million pounds of wool in one week.

In the 1950s the American Woolen Company closed down and in 1959 one wing of the Wood Mill was razed. A few years later, the remaining building began housing electronics and technology firms.

Construction of the Ayer Mills, named for William Wood's father-in-law, began in 1909 at the corner of Merrimack and South Union Streets. Manufacturing began in 1910, just a few years after the Wood Mill—seen here next to the Duck Bridge—was finished. The two mills faced each other across South Union Street and were connected by an underground tunnel.

Crowned by a high tower with a weathervane 267 feet above street level, the Ayer Mill evoked the powerful image of its parent, the American Woolen Company. Its clock truly ruled the city, the bell tolling the time for many years until it fell silent and disappeared. In 1992 citizens funded a restoration of the clock and had a new bell cast. Today the Ayer Mill clock, the largest mill clock in the world, once again keeps time for Lawrence.

Uswoco Worsted Mills,
Lawrence, Mass.

The United States Worsted Company's main building was built here on South Broadway, near the South Canal. At the time of its construction in 1908, Lawrence was experiencing a mill building boom larger than any ever seen in a textile city before.

Beginning with the construction of the Wood Mill in 1905, new mills—and substantial additions to existing ones—began springing up at a dizzying pace that lasted for a decade. Still more expansion followed World War I.

By 1924, almost 300 acres of the city were covered with textile mills, most standing shoulder to shoulder along the river and canals, as can be seen in this c. 1945 photograph. To the left of the Merrimack River, proceeding upwards, are buildings of the Washington, Pemberton, Duck, and Kunhardt Mills, and the Hamblet Machine Co. To the left of Canal Street are the Everett Mills and Champion International. Crossing over the Spicket River, on Marston Street, the Patchogue-Plymouth Mills are followed by the Lawrence Gas and Electric Co.

At right, proceeding upwards on the south side of the river, are structures belonging to E. Frank Lewis Wool Scouring, the Lawrence Gas and Electric Co., the Ayer and Wood Mills, and the Pacific Print Works.

Three

The City Grows Up

When Lawrence officially became a town in the spring of 1847, its municipal needs were few. A town meeting on April 30 of that year voted to build two schools, purchase two fire engines, and expend $1,200 on the upkeep and repair of roads and bridges.

It wasn't long, of course, until Lawrence had greater needs: parks; a water system; more roads and bridges; buildings to house municipal offices, courts—and prisoners. A city was growing up.

The above image is an architect's rendering of the Essex County Court House on the corner of Common and Appleton Streets, c. 1902.

City Hall, designed in the classical style, was erected in 1849. Although the building housed municipal offices, it was used primarily as a public hall in the early years—the only one in the area large enough to accommodate sizable numbers of people. Dances, concerts, lectures, dog shows, fairs, theatricals, military drills, funerals, and religious services were regularly held here.

This illustration shows what the hall looked like in January 1860, when it was being used as a hospital and morgue for victims of the Pemberton Mill disaster.

One of the facility's drawbacks was a notorious echo that tormented speakers and listeners alike—a problem tamed somewhat when draperies were hung on the walls to absorb sound. In 1872 more improvements were made, including the addition of a new stage, scenery, lighting, and galleries. Further renovations followed in 1877.

In 1848 John M. Smith, a town selectman and Essex Company employee, designed and carved the wooden eagle that still reigns over City Hall today. Shown here c. 1923 with two unidentified workmen perched next to it, the eagle is over 9 feet tall from bill to tail. The pedestal and ball were also carved by Smith, bringing the bird's total cost to $500.

While municipal government and its corresponding bureaucracy grew substantially in the seventy-plus years after 1849, City Hall did not. So in 1923, local architect George G. Adams was hired to remodel and enlarge the building.

Although Adams worked assiduously to retain as much of the history as possible, little of the original structure is visible today. The public hall, scene of so many memorable events over the years, was replaced by two floors of offices, and a skylight-topped rotunda was created in the center of the building. This photograph of the remodeled edifice was taken from the intersection of Common and Appleton Streets.

45

Of all the talented architects who have left their mark on Lawrence, perhaps none is remembered with such admiration and awe as George G. Adams (1850–1932). This book contains a number of Adams' most outstanding designs, including the Rollins School, the Massachusetts State Armory, the Lawrence Police Station, the Colonial Theater, and the Bay State Building.

Although he worked in various architectural styles throughout his long career, Adams is best known in this city for his Richardson Romanesque structures, such as the Lawrence Public Library.

Opened in 1892 at the corner of Haverhill and Hampshire Streets, the library was built on land owned and donated by Judge Daniel Appleton White, whose White Fund still provides monies annually toward both the library and a free public lecture series. Funds for the library building itself came as a gift in memory of Nathaniel G. White—a lawyer and former library trustee—from his wife and daughter. The two White families were not related.

To accommodate the water needs of residents living at higher locations in Lawrence, and to insure sufficient high pressure for fighting fires, the city authorized construction of a high-service water system.

Built in 1896 near the intersection of Hillside Avenue and Yale Street on Tower Hill, the standpipe, containing 9 tons of rivets and nearly 137 tons of steel, was designed by city engineer Arthur D. Marble to hold more than 500,000 gallons of water when full.

Residents deemed the structure most unattractive and the decision was made to encase it in an ornamental brick tower. Designed by Lawrence architect George G. Adams, the octagonal tower is the tallest building in the city and boasts an observation balcony 107 feet above its foundation. It abuts Lawrence reservoir (not pictured), which is capable of storing over 40 million gallons of water in an area 700 feet long by 400 feet wide.

High Service Tower, Lawrence. Mass.

In 1848, for a consideration of $1, the Essex Company deeded 17 1/2 acres of land for a common to the residents of Lawrence, on the condition that it "be forever kept open as a place of public recreation and resort."

The Soldiers and Sailors Monument, erected on the common in 1881 and seen here in 1898, honors the more than 2,000 Lawrencians who served in the Civil War. Monuments, plaques, and statuary honoring those who served in America's other wars can be found all over the city.

The Lawrence Common was renamed Campagnone Common in 1951 for three Lawrence brothers killed within a four-month period at the end of World War II. This memorial, chosen by Gold Star Mothers and dedicated in 1949, honors all the men and women from Lawrence who fought in that war. Of the 12,000 who served, over 300 died.

The Massachusetts State Armory, shown here *c.* 1905, stood at the corner of Amesbury and Methuen Streets. Dedicated in 1893 and demolished in the early 1970s, it was used by the militia and national guard. Besides containing office space and training facilities, the building also held an impressive arsenal. During the Lawrence Textile Strike of 1912, the Armory served as headquarters for many of the military and paramilitary units assigned here to deal with protesting strikers.

One of the oldest correctional facilities in the state, the Essex County Jail on Auburn Street was constructed in 1853, with various improvements and additions made over the years. Always controversial, several fires of late have rendered the jail uninhabitable. This photograph was taken around 1890.

Until 1867, when the Lawrence Police Station (left) was constructed on the southwest corner of Lawrence and Common Streets, wooden lock-ups were used to confine offenders until they could be tried. Even City Hall served as a lock-up in its early days. Besides containing cells and offices, the Lawrence Police Station boasted a police court and a hall once used as an armory.

In 1914 the mansard-roofed building was demolished to make room for a more modern and commodious facility on the same site. Seen in this c. 1920 photograph, the new station served the city for over fifty years until it, too, was razed. The present station, located on Lowell Street, was erected in the 1970s.

Lawrence appropriated funds for its first two fire engines in 1847. Driving a fire truck in the days before motorization often required the strength to handle several horses at a time, as shown in this 1903 view of a ladder truck on Broadway near the intersection of Cross and Holly Streets. Around the time of World War I, Lawrence became famous nationally for its four-horse hitch, the only such team in the United States.

By the early 1920s the Lawrence Fire Department became fully motorized and fire horses were put to work for other city departments. The vehicles proudly displayed here, outside the old Central Fire Station at 80 Lowell Street, were manufactured by Stutz Motor Company. This c. 1922 photograph, taken by photographer George H. Leck of Lawrence, was used by Stutz in a national ad campaign.

Boston and Maine's North Station, off Essex Street near the intersection of Broadway, was the elegant grande dame of the three railroad stations existing in Lawrence in the late nineteenth century. Built in 1878 and demolished completely by the early 1930s, this depot served well over one hundred passenger trains per day.

The Franklin House, originally called Coburn's, was among the very first hotels built in Lawrence. Constructed by the Essex Company in 1847 and remodeled several times over the years, it was conveniently located on Broadway, across from North Station. In 1908—when the hotel offered two separate dining rooms and seventy-five sleeping rooms—accommodations at the Franklin cost between $2 and $3 per night, including meals. The structure was demolished in the 1960s, a casualty of urban redevelopment.

In 1907 the Boston & Maine Railroad Station, Southern Division, stood facing Canal Street between Amesbury and Lawrence Streets, where Blotner's and Eidam's parking lots are situated today. Trains reached the station via a railroad bridge over the Merrimack, located approximately where the Central Bridge is now. All that remains of that bridge today is the portion shown here, now open to motor vehicle traffic entering Canal Street over the North Canal, en route to Lawrence Street.

Part of the old Essex Yard as it appeared in the 1920s, looking northwesterly from the Upper Pacific Mills. A small portion of the huge Boston & Maine rail yard is visible at the right. The buildings with the enormous smokestacks were part of the Pacific Mills Power Plant.

Today, Lawton's Hot Dog Stand sits at the intersection of Broadway and Canal Streets, which can be seen in the lower right corner of the photograph.

The old Lawrence Post Office, built in 1905 on the northwest corner of Broadway and Essex Streets, was demolished in 1971. The mailmen in 1908 were, from left to right: (front row) James C. Curran, Eugene Trudeau, Frank E. Osgood, Edwin H. Colby, Herbert May, Honorable Louis S. Cox (postmaster), J. Rodney Ball (assistant postmaster), Daniel J. Murray, Abard Welton, Clarence Austin, and Walter A. Singer; (second row) Daniel S. Barry, John J. Garvey, Thomas Murphy, William J. Kennedy, John W. Lynch, Henry T. Sutcliffe, Henry A. Lynch, William A. Gleason, William Cyr, Augustine Sullivan, John J. Healey, Domenic P. Flanagan, Joseph W. Seed, John A. Keating, Walter A. Morse, Robert Silke, George Sumner, and John A. McManus; (third row) Sylvester J. Sheehan, John A. O'Brien, Emile R. Spalke, Thomas J. McHugh, Frank J. Seiferth, John J. Costello, Albert Rawnsley, Charles A. McQueeney, and Timothy J. Dineen; (back row) Joseph T. McEvoy, Charles J. Riordan, Alfred Butterworth, James O'Brien, John J. Ford, Joseph Barry, substitute carrier Mulvey, and Thomas A. Sullivan.

One of the most controversial public projects in Lawrence history was the construction of the Central Bridge, begun in 1914 and completed four years later. Replacing a railroad bridge and linking South Lawrence with downtown at Amesbury Street, the project also required the building of two smaller spans to cross the canals at either end of Central Bridge. In the early 1980s major improvements were made.

In Lawrence's early days, drinking water came from wells and cisterns. In 1872 the city decided to build a municipal water system, drawing water from the Merrimack River. For the first twenty years after the water works was established, however, there was no water purification system.

In 1893 Hiram Mills—the Essex Company engineer who founded the Lawrence Experiment Station—designed filter beds employing a slow-sand filtration process. Occupying 2 1/2 acres on Water Street, the filters—the first of their kind in the country—greatly aided in the control of deadly diseases from river water, especially typhoid fever. This c. 1906 photograph was taken during the expansion of the system, when a new covered filter bed was being installed.

1901 ICE 1901

CASH PRICES.

30 pounds,	10 cents.
50 pounds,	15 cents.
100 pounds,	20 cents.

100 to 300 pounds at one delivery,	20c per 100 lbs.	
300 to 1000 pounds at one delivery,	15c "	"
1000 pounds or more at one delivery,	12 1-2c "	"

Shaved or chopped ice, 15c per basket.

BY SCORE.

Less than 50 pounds at one delivery,	30c per 100 lbs.	
50 to 100 pounds at one delivery,	25c "	"
100 to 300 pounds at one delivery,	20c "	"
300 to 1000 pounds at one delivery,	15c "	"
1000 pounds or more at one delivery,	12 1-2c "	"

Shaved or chopped ice, 15c per basket.

All ice sold by weight.

No less than 10 cents' worth of ice carried into houses.

Ice at the ice-house same price as from wagons.

No ice delivered on Sunday.

All bills due the first day of each month.

Drivers are not allowed to change above prices or make contracts or rules other than these.

$1.00, $2.00, $5.00 and $10.00 coupon books for sale at the OFFICE at a discount of 10 per cent.

Customers will confer a favor by reporting to the office immediately any cause for complaint. Corrections cannot be made at the end of the season.

LAWRENCE ICE COMPANY,

253 Essex Street, Lawrence Mass.

Mystic Pond, Methuen, Mass., Telephone 218-5.

Among Lawrence's little known yet exceptionally important businesses in the nineteenth century was the cutting and sale of ice.

The photograph below shows ice on the Merrimack River, just below the old pumping station, being prepared for cutting. Ice houses—where cut ice was stored in sawdust to keep it frozen—were familiar sites on both sides of the river.

In the days before electric refrigeration, some of the ice cut in Lawrence was shipped by train out of the city, but most was consumed right here in businesses, industries, and homes. Home orders were usually placed by displaying a large card, printed with the number of pounds desired, in the front window. The ice man, driving by in his wagon, would then be able to just look up, see the card, and deliver that amount right to the door.

The Cross Coal Company, seen here in about 1933, was established by the Cross family in the 1880s. The company's yard and coal pocket were located on Railroad Street, next to the B&M Railroad tracks. Here both anthracite and bituminous coal were off-loaded from rail cars, then processed for delivery throughout Greater Lawrence. Today this is the home of the Whaleco Oil Company.

Because central heating systems were costly to install, especially in multi-family two and three-deckers, many homes in Lawrence depended on a kitchen range for heating well into the twentieth century.

Thomas A. Emmons arrived here in 1868, and soon established the Emmons Loom Harness Company on May Street. Like many other businesses in Lawrence, the company was not a producer of cloth but was textile related, supplying necessary equipment to the mills. This photograph illustrates the enormity of the operation at the height of its prosperity.

Although few of these structures remain today, one—the May Street Spring—does endure. Owing its existence directly to Mr. Emmons, the spring continues to provide water to the public today, thanks greatly to the Haffner/Fournier family.

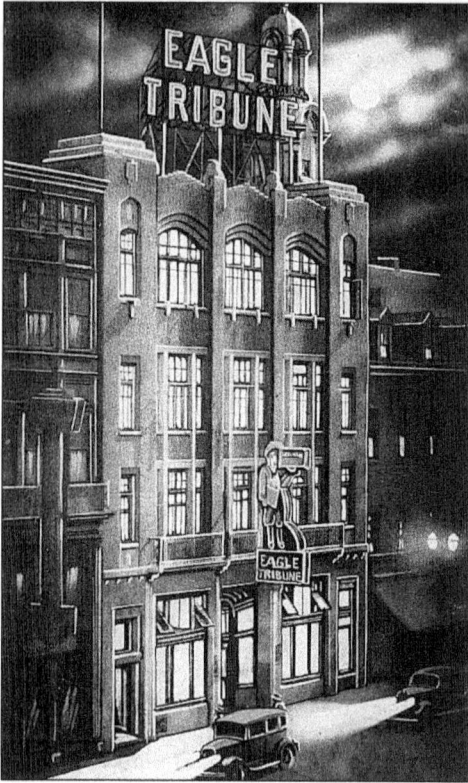

The *Eagle Tribune* remains Lawrence's oldest continuing newspaper. Begun as the *Evening Tribune* in 1890, it has been owned by the Rogers family since 1898. At left is a 1930s view of the paper's stylish headquarters at 279–285 Essex Street. The famed 14-foot neon newsboy brightened up the thoroughfare from 1930 until the company moved to its present location in North Andover in 1968.

Many residents remember crowding outside the building's first-floor windows to read the "bulletin board," a 3-foot wide, up-to-the-minute news display. Rarely could anyone walk by without being caught up in the events of the day.

Lawrence's first newspaper, the *Merrimack Courier*, appeared in 1846, before the "new city" had officially received a name. As was the case with all Lawrence papers before the 1860s, it was issued weekly.

Here, *Tribune* newsboys wait to unload the evening papers for delivery, c. 1955. Home delivery was uncommon prior to World War I. Instead, people purchased their newspapers on Essex Street, at mill gates, on street corners, and in offices.

Four

Body, Mind, and Spirit

Tuberculosis Hospital, Lawrence, Mass.

The Essex Company was determined to preserve small-town virtues by making sure that the labor force was properly housed and that intellectual and spiritual needs were addressed.

With the ever increasing flood of immigrants, however, the model town soon became an immigrant city. Tenement districts were crowded and unsanitary, education was neglected in favor of child labor, and diseases like tuberculosis became common.

The Tuberculosis Hospital, established in 1909 on Chickering Street in South Lawrence, treated and nursed patients who had been cared for earlier in a day camp at the General Hospital. The facility's large windows and balconies offered the fresh air and sunshine that was the preferred form of treatment at that time.

Although originally trained as a physician, Dr. George Packard entered the ministry in 1844, arriving in Lawrence in 1846 to become the first rector of Grace Church. He was active in every aspect of the parish until his death in 1876.

A decisive, concerned, and inspirational leader, Packard's influence extended beyond his own church. Among his many accomplishments was the co-founding of the Lawrence Provident Association, later known as the City Mission and then as Family Service of Greater Lawrence, which was established to assist the "worthy poor" of the community. Education was also of paramount importance to Packard; he served on the school committee and also became the superintendent of Lawrence schools. The Packard School bears his name.

The Protectory Of Mary Immaculate was founded in 1868 by Reverend James Taaffe, then pastor at the Immaculate Conception Church.

Located at the intersection of White and Maple Streets, it was the earliest and most important Roman Catholic charitable institution in the city. Administered by the Grey Nuns of Montreal since its inception, the Protectory provided vital services to the poor, destitute, and infirm, with particular attention given to orphans and the elderly. Today, in its new quarters, the Mary Immaculate Restorative Center still provides for the aged.

"Taking the pledge" was a rather common individual gesture for many in the nineteenth century. Various temperance societies were organized here in Lawrence as early as 1846, with the evils of strong drink proclaimed vigorously by both Protestant and Catholic leaders. What makes this card especially interesting is that, while most pledges stressed abstinence from alcohol, this one addressed a fairly comprehensive assortment of evils.

Olive Plant Sunday School,
AND
A BAND OF HOPE.
ORGANIZED, SEPTEMBER 16TH, 1855.

This is to Certify, That

Is a member of this School and Band, and has taken the following
PLEDGE:

I Pledge myself not to use any Intoxicating Liquors as a beverage, or Tobacco in any way. I also pledge myself not to Swear, Lie, or Steal.

Pledge Book Keeper.

Lawrence, ... 185 .

PLACE OF MEETING,
FIRST CHRISTIAN CHURCH,
COMMON STREET.

A major inquiry into the living conditions in Lawrence during the first decade of the twentieth century was published in the year 1912. *The Lawrence Survey*, supported solely by money from the White Fund, provided a detailed report on the deplorable housing conditions affecting large numbers of residents, especially immigrants living on the north side. Several areas held from 300 to 600 people per acre, competing with Harlem in New York City for the highest population density in the country.

This residence on the corner of Lawrence and Valley Streets was home to the Nathaniel G. White family, donors of the Lawrence Public Library. The house was deeded by Mrs. White, after the death of her husband, to the Lawrence YWCA. In this building the Y evolved from a small agency attracting primarily Protestant girls into a large multi-service organization serving immigrant women and their families.

In 1913 the YWCA branched out and opened the International Institute at 52 Union Street in a building donated by the textile manufacturers. By 1919 several neighborhood centers had been established—including this one at 316 Market Street in South Lawrence—where English, sewing, cooking, and canning classes were held. Many club meetings and parties were also popular diversions for the foreign factory girls.

In 1909 young Pittsburgh steel heiress Helen Clay Frick began to offer free two-week vacations in Wenham to selected working girls from Lawrence, Lowell, Lynn, and Boston. The camaraderie experienced that first summer led to the establishment of True Blue clubs in the girls' hometowns.

Miss Frick paid the rent for a year-round club room in the Gleason Building and continued offering free annual Wenham vacations to True Blue members until the 1950s. From left to right are Marion Broadley, Ethel Davis, Ella Barnet, Emma Briggs, Esther West, Sophie Yunggebauer, and Ivy Fickenwirth.

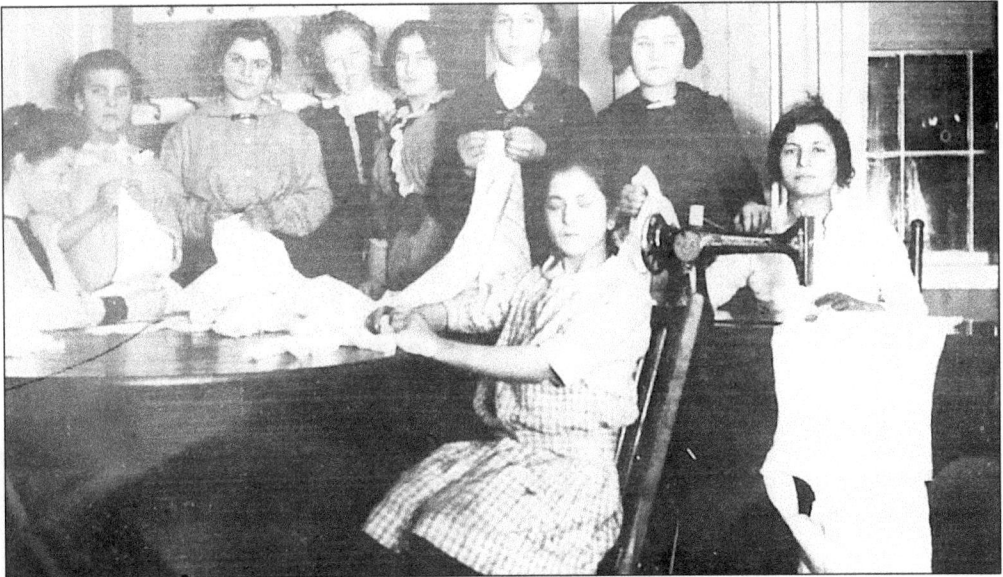

The International Institute was committed to aiding the immigrant girl "from the moment she enters American life." Instruction was provided not only in English, but also in clothing, cooking, child care, and American customs. Classes in sewing and millinery, like the one here for Italians in 1915, were especially popular because they made it possible for immigrant girls to at least "look American."

Slowly the International Institute began serving Italians, Poles, and Lithuanians. These young ladies, shown c. 1919, became the first Syrians—actually Lebanese—to be attracted to this activity center in their neighborhood. The Institute also provided a supervised playground in its backyard, a rare service at a time when so many mothers were working in the mills and no adult was around to mind the little ones.

This 1938 image shows a group of International Institute youngsters dressed in their native costumes to present "The Pageant of Nations" at the Junior Red Cross Rally in Salem. Their names truly represent the immigrant population of Lawrence. From left to right are: (front row) Peter Kalitka, Walter Melnicki, John Borys, and Peter Nemerowski; (back row) Kiki Kutsulianos, Isabel Ulozas, Margaret Ulozas, Marion Paboojian, Anne Terlecks, Jane Jackowski, Verna Weigel, Ilona Korziuk, Eva Ziza, Marion Archetti, Wanda Sarna, Genevieve Assaf, and Mary Manianos.

Learning English was the most important and often the most difficult task for "foreigners," as new immigrants were called. Language skills made it possible to move into better jobs, make new friends, and someday become a U.S. Citizen. This 1915 photograph shows an International Institute English class for young Lithuanian women.

In the early 1880s the first Jewish immigrants arrived in Lawrence and established their neighborhood, or "Shtetel," around Common, Valley, Concord, and Lowell Streets, where Jewish stores were found among the tenements.

Soon synagogues and "shuls" took care of the religious needs of the Jewish community, teaching Hebrew as part of religious education. Some families also had their children enrolled in Yiddish classes, like this one about 1925, to learn the language spoken for generations by Jewish people in Eastern Europe.

Like many of her pupils at the Walton School—built in 1862 at the corner of Methuen and Newbury Streets—Miss Stoddard lived in a nearby mill boarding house. Notice that her 1883 class was clearly well behaved and obviously came prepared for a photo session, with many wearing their "Sunday best."

At that time virtually all principals and teachers in Lawrence were women, except for masters and sub-masters at the Packard, Oliver, and High Schools. Women teachers could not marry without forfeiting their jobs.

Since 1859 the Sisters of Notre Dame de Namur have been in Lawrence teaching at St. Mary's School, the first formal Catholic school in the city operated by a religious order.

In September 1880, "old" St. Mary's Church, shown here situated across Haverhill Street from the present edifice, was remodeled to house the school.

The first class of girls enrolled at the Holy Rosary School in 1910 posed for this photograph with their teachers, Venerini Sisters Augusta Setaccioli and Rosina Vagni. The school was located in the church basement on the corner of Union and Essex Streets.

In 1909 four Venerini Sisters arrived in Boston from Naples. They were greeted at the landing by Reverend Mariano Milanese, pastor of Holy Rosary Church in Lawrence. They soon established their first mission in America in Lawrence, designed to serve the Italian immigrant community.

In September 1935 the Marist Brothers, under the leadership of Brother Florentius, founded Central Catholic, the first Roman Catholic high school for young men in Lawrence.

Classes were held initially in the Knights of Columbus building on Haverhill Street. Additional space was soon needed and was found at the old Franklin and Hampshire Street Schools, as well as in a portion of Holy Trinity School. In 1938 this building, now demolished, was constructed on Auburn Street. The present school on Hampshire Street, built 1970–71, continues Central's original commitment to excellence in education.

The Lawrence school system was carefully planned in 1848 after consultation with education reformer Horace Mann. The large number of immigrants with no English skills and the need for many children to go to work required a very flexible educational system. Lawrence soon became known for its innovative programs and for its success in teaching all ages—in many languages.

The above photograph shows the Oliver School and the old Lawrence High School building on Haverhill Street, *c*. 1898. Today, Oliver Junior High occupies most of this site.

The present Lawrence High has been enlarged several times since first opening its doors on Haverhill and Lawrence Streets in 1901. Among LHS graduates are actress Thelma Todd, composer George Whitefield Chadwick, Nobel Prize winner Elias Corey, and internationally-acclaimed poet Robert Frost. Frost, who wrote for the school's *Bulletin,* was co-valedictorian in 1892 with Elinor Miriam White, who would soon become his wife.

68

Emily Greene Wetherbee was a member of the Lawrence High School faculty and one of the most beloved teachers and admired women in Lawrence. She wrote poetry and gave public readings, spoke at most civic events, and saw her oratory reprinted in newspapers for all to read. Miss Wetherbee, shown here in 1887, was a perfect example of a well-educated woman of the Victorian age who cared for her pupils and loved her city.

The Emily G. Wetherbee School on Newton Street in South Lawrence opened its doors one hundred years ago. While the original interior spaces and woodwork still look well preserved, the stairs are worn from the footprints of the many little feet that have climbed them.

DRS.

Boynton and Boynton,

Treat and Cure all Chronic
Diseases of Men and
Women.

Fifteen years experience enables
them to make quick cures.

CONSULTATION FREE.

Professional calls made to all parts
of the city night or day.

260 Broadway, Lawren.e, Mass
and 537 Essex St., Room 14.

DR. BOYNTON

MRS. DR. BOYNTON.

This is an 1889 advertisement for one of the very first husband and wife medical teams to practice together in Lawrence. Dr. Edwin W. Boynton and his wife, Dr. Stella W. Boynton (a cancer specialist), lived at 260 Broadway when this ad appeared. Female practitioners had been in Lawrence virtually since the community's beginning; most specialized in treating women.

Dr. Arthur I. Teutonico, the first Lawrence dentist of Italian descent, is pictured in his office, c. 1924. An Italian immigrant, Teutonico arrived in Lawrence before the turn of the century, receiving his primary education in the city's schools before attending Phillips Academy and then Tufts University. A highly-regarded member of a number of social, religious, and professional organizations, Dr. Teutonico resided with his family at 38 Newton Street until his death in 1949.

Wood Home for Aged People, Lawrence, Mass.

The Wood Home for the Aged, located on Berkeley Street on Clover Hill, is now called the Berkeley Retirement Home. Before it got that name, it was known for many years as the Lawrence Home for the Aged. The handsome brick structure was built in 1909 on land donated by Edward F. Searles of Methuen.

The original Wood Home stood on the corner of Bailey and Blanchard Streets in South Lawrence. It was donated by the William Wood family—who also built the Wood Memorial Free Baptist Chapel on Coolidge Street.

The entrance to the Burke Hospital on Marston Street in 1940. Originally the site of the city's almshouse during Lawrence's early years, this site was later known, successively, as Cottage Hospital and the Lawrence Municipal Hospital. In 1936 it was named for Bessie M. Burke, one of the institution's most distinguished matrons, well known for her unceasing dedication to the poor and needy. Before its demise in the late 1970s, the institution cared primarily for Lawrence's chronically ill. Its closing caused considerable controversy.

The Russell Paper Company, whose stone storehouse on the corner of Marston and Canal Streets still stands, was the earliest paper mill in Lawrence. It began operations in 1853 under the ownership of father and son William and William A. Russell. Because paper manufacturing used cotton, linen, and other fiber rags back then, paper mills were often located near textile manufacturers. The industry continued to be a major force in Lawrence even after wood pulp was introduced to paper manufacturing.

William A. Russell died in 1899, leaving his Prospect Hill estate to the Ladies Union Charitable Society. The society had formed in 1875 for the purpose of establishing a hospital in Lawrence. The first building obtained by the group to serve as the Lawrence General Hospital was at 95 Methuen Street, where the first patient was admitted in February 1881.

The Russell estate provided the larger quarters the hospital had grown to need, and by 1904 the "new" General Hospital opened its doors.

This building on Howard Street atop Prospect Hill housed the Children's Home of the Lawrence General Hospital from 1908 to 1912. After that it became the German Old Folks Home—its name reflecting the community it was established to serve. The German Home still operates as a nursing home for the elderly today.

With advances in medical science, the demand for hospital space continued to grow. This 1940s aerial view of the Lawrence General Hospital shows the many additions made to the former Russell estate in just forty years. The Russell Trust Fund still helps support the hospital today.

The Clover Hill Hospital on Berkeley Street was founded by Drs. Nicandro F. and Frank DeCesare and Dr. Angelo Calderone. By 1953, when the facility celebrated its 30th anniversary, some 12,000 babies of all colors and creeds had been delivered here. Eventually the Clover Hill Hospital was phased out; the building still stands, however, and is once again a residence.

Some of the Greater Lawrence physicians practicing at Clover Hill during the 1950s. From left to right are: (front row) Eugene E. Guilmette, Joseph Gurry, Herbert Coulson, John McDermott, John Oddy, Joseph Bradley, Nicandro DeCesare, Adolph DeNuccio, and Santo Quartarone; (second row) George Lemaitre Sr., Andrew F. Shea, Paul Oskar Sr., Richard Neil, John D'Urso, Joseph DiSalvo, James Seccareccio, Philip Bretts, and Stanley Chart; (third row) Charles Lee, John McArdle Jr., H. Frank McCarthy, Joseph Pinchesky, Harry Kellett, Philip Zanfagna, John Wholey, Frederick Atkinson, unknown, and Frank DeCesare; (fourth row) Joseph Barbieri, James Hindman, Joseph Calitri, Nicholas Zannini, Herbert Cregg, Joseph Boyle, Lionel St. Louis, and Salvatore Barone; (back row) Peter McKinnis, William Land, Morris Grossman, Frank Hayden, James Pash, Martin J. Shannon, John Barry, George Desmet, and Joseph Gurka.

Five

Essex Street

As word spread about the building of the "new city," enterprising merchants began arriving to set up shop, undeterred by the fact that retail space was virtually nonexistent. One of the earliest arrivals was Amos Pillsbury, who came from Georgetown in the spring of 1846.

Unable to find an available building to house his boot and shoe business, Pillsbury simply set up operations on a gondola anchored below Andover Bridge. When cold weather set in later that year, he moved to a newly-constructed wooden store on Essex Street. Downtown shopping had begun.

By the time Frank A. Hiscox opened his store at 496 Essex about fifty-five years later, Pillsbury wouldn't have recognized the place. For the French-Canadian ladies on this omnibus, and thousands of others, Essex Street was now *the* place to meet, greet, and be seen.

The handsome brick buildings lining Essex Street today got their start in early 1847, when ground was broken for what became known as Merchants Row, the first brick mercantile block on Essex Street.

Others soon followed, their buildings much less modest than those of Merchants Row. Two early brick blocks are shown here: the above photograph is of the Old Pemberton Block, extending easterly from the intersection of Pemberton and Essex Streets, as it looked in about 1858; the photograph below is of the City Block, c. 1860, located at the intersection of Essex and Lawrence Streets, where the Bay State Building stands today.

ESSEX STREET in 1873

At first, development on Essex Street took place only on the street's north side, which may have been because there was more sunlight available to stores facing south. It wasn't until the widespread introduction of the incandescent lamp that substantial building began taking place on the south side of Essex, replacing a grassy field known as the Corporation Reserve. The reserve, seen here on the left in 1873, ran from Broadway to Union Street. It was used for everything from grazing cows to holding circuses.

At right is the Appleton Block, constructed in the Italianate style by Nathan Appleton in 1854. Today, Shawmut Bank occupies the space where J.C. Wadleigh was located.

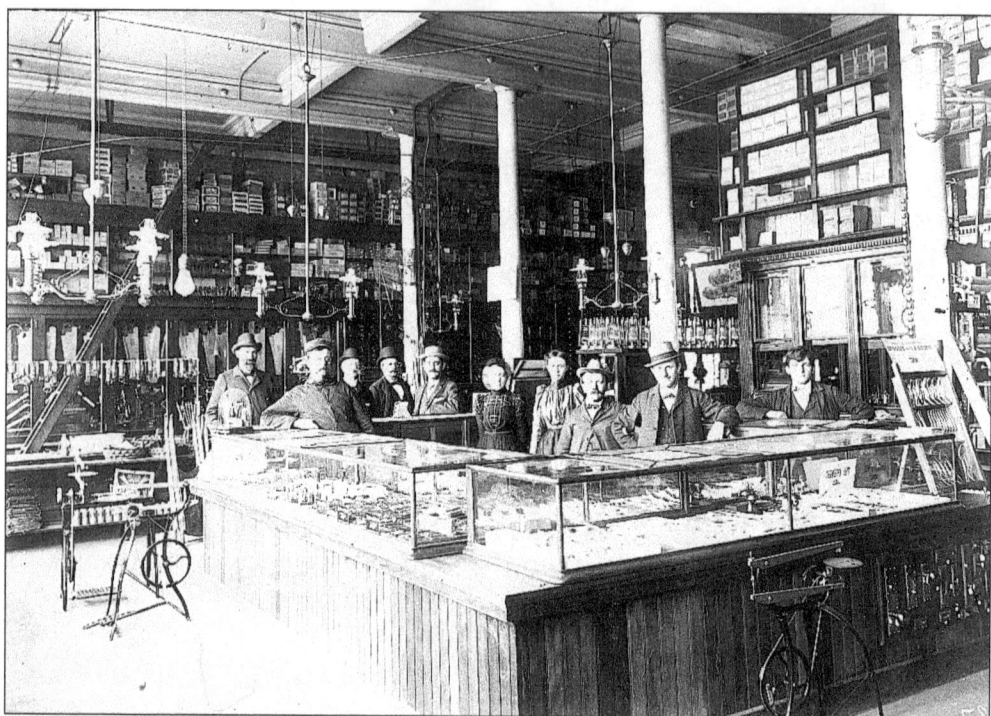

Established in 1859, Treat Hardware, seen above c. 1900, is the city's oldest continuously operating hardware store. For many years it was housed in the Brechin Block, shown below as it appeared in the 1890s.

Named for a town in Scotland from which many immigrants came in the nineteenth century, this massive building once occupied the southeast corner of Essex Street and Broadway. Besides Treat's, Brechin Block also contained the Broadway Savings Bank, the Lawrence Light Infantry, the Lawrence National Bank, A.M. Fay Insurance, and the Lawrence Co-operative Bank. On March 14, 1924, fire destroyed the building.

Essex Street, looking west from the intersection of Hampshire Street in 1893, looks much different than it does today. The building at right in the foreground is where the art deco Woolworth Building now stands. Beyond it is the Bicknell Brothers' clock and the Blakely Building. Across the street is Chin Lee's, one of many Chinese laundries once found in Lawrence. Note the double set of trolley tracks; Broadway had them too.

The Bicknell Brothers moved into spectacular new quarters at 467–471 Essex Street in 1879. Besides manufacturing and selling the most fashionable clothes available, the store became a tourist attraction—known far and wide for its fancy interior, elaborate window displays, and exquisite street clock. Advertising and promotion were a Bicknell specialty, as seen here in 1904 when local children posed for a store promotion. The young boy standing at left is Irving E. Hinton, who grew up to become vice president of Bay State Merchant's National Bank.

Tea and butter stores, forerunners of today's convenience marts, were a common sight in the early twentieth century. Many people can still remember running in to Kennedy's or Vermont Tea and Butter to pick up butter or cheese cut from a round wooden tub.

Kennedy's Butter, Tea and Coffee stores operated in Lawrence from 1899 until 1947, opening first at 169 Essex Street. By the 1930s, the company had three locations in the city—two on Essex Street and one on Broadway. This photograph was taken in one of their Lawrence stores about 1920. Do you know which one?

In the background of this photograph of the 1903 Veteran Firemen's Parade, at 141 Essex Street, is Elias Kapelson's clothing store for men and boys. Kapelson, a Jewish immigrant, came to Lawrence from Lithuania. His son David founded Kap's, a prominent Lawrence clothing store—and an elegant fixture on Essex Street until its departure from the city a few years ago.

This mechanical advertising kiosk once stood in front of the H.M. Whitney apothecary shop at 297 Essex Street (see p. 76). Approximately 6 feet tall, with a revolving cylinder, the device was illuminated and made quite a sight after dark. It was operated by a spring motor that required winding every twenty-four hours.

Kiosks promoting local businesses, products, and services were not only quite common along Essex Street at the turn of the century, but were a large part of the thoroughfare's attraction as well. Merchants then, as today, prided themselves on the distinctive quality of their ad gadgets and displays—and both shopper and visitor responded by returning again and again.

Charles E. Scheffler maintained his pharmacy in the Ordway Block, at the northeast corner of Essex and Franklin Streets. The Ordway is one of the oldest business blocks on this section of Essex Street. Notice the insect powders in this 1903 window display? Most of life's problems are, indeed, timeless.

This spectacular photograph of Essex Street, looking east from near Amesbury, was taken in October 1912, at the time of the God and Country Parade (discussed in more detail on p. 94). At left stands the distinctive Gleason Building, with S.S. Kresge's 5&10¢ store to its right.

Across the street is the Opera House, also remembered as the Winter Garden; the Central Building and the Odd Fellows Block can be seen beyond. Across Lawrence Street, the Bay State Building dominates the background; seen from this angle, even City Hall is dwarfed by its presence.

Bay State was Lawrence's first bank, receiving its charter in 1847. Like many financial institutions in the city, it began as a mill bank; Charles S. Storrow served as its first president. In business on the northeast corner of Essex and Lawrence Streets from its beginning, Bay State decided, at the turn of the century, to replace its old building with an elaborate new one. The result was this handsome eight-story edifice, designed by local architect George G. Adams.

Shown here soon after its completion in 1905, the Bay State was the tallest office building in Lawrence and perhaps the largest between Boston and Canada. Because it quickly became the most desirable professional address in the city, adjacent land was purchased and the building was enlarged in 1912.

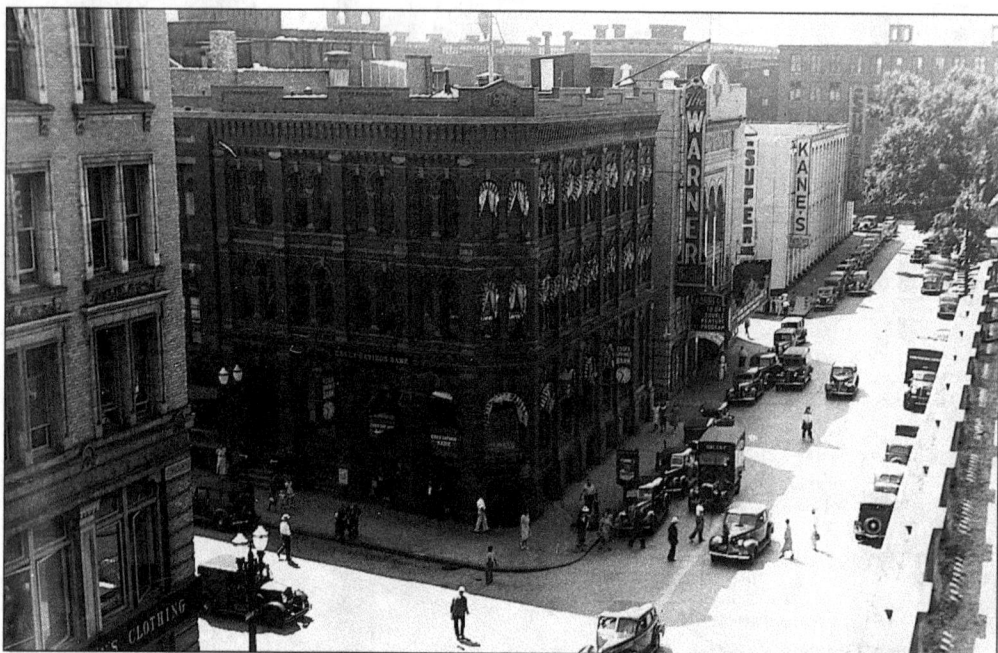

This late 1930s view, looking southeast from the busy intersection of Essex and Lawrence Streets, shows just a corner of the Bay State Building at the left. Across Essex Street is the Essex Savings Bank, the first savings bank in the city and, at one time, the largest bank in Essex County; behind it, facing Lawrence Street, is the Warner Theater—now a parking lot. The building housing the Super Store eventually became Jo-Gal Shoe Company, which was demolished in 1994.

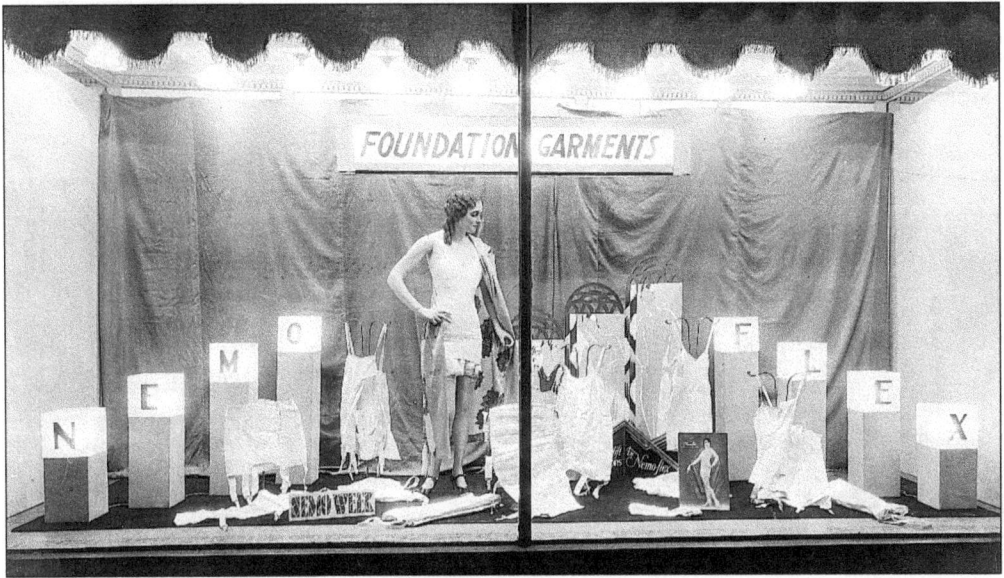

Lawrence's largest department store, A.B. Sutherland Co., was located near the northwest corner of Essex and Lawrence Streets. Shown here in the early 1930s, the store boasted four floors, thirty-five departments, and a twice-a-day home delivery service renowned for cheerfully depositing even single spools of thread on shoppers' doorsteps. Part of the fun of strolling Essex Street was a walk by Sutherland's window displays, one of which is shown above in 1928. And who can forget the maze of brass tubes at the selling counters—magically transporting money and receipts?

Sheathed in scaffolding, City Hall received its major facelift in 1923. Many of the buildings lining the right-hand side of Essex Street, east of Franklin, have now vanished. The Ordway Block and the Blakely Building, on the left, are still prominent landmarks today.

Looking east toward Union Street and the Everett Mill in the early 1920s, it is possible to get a sense of just how crowded with people the sidewalks often were. Essex Street was not only a route taken to get somewhere else, it was also a destination all its own.

This c. 1895 photograph provides a peek inside an Essex Street millinery shop. Usually owned by women, hat shops were small worlds of finery and grace—places where shoppers would not so much browse as be "attended to," often by the milliner herself. Personal attention was anticipated and expected—especially by the four-legged shopper in the foreground!

After emigrating from San Antonio, Sicily, in 1912, Antonio Leone, like many Lawrence immigrants, worked in the textile mills before going into business for himself. He poses proudly here, c. 1920, behind the soda fountain of his rented store. Antonio Leone Cigars and Tobacco was located at 87 Essex Street, on the corner of Newbury; Mr. Leone finally bought the building in 1952.

Trolleys—shown here escorting a circus parade down Essex Street—were an important mode of transportation around and about the city. Although street railways began here in the 1860s, the transition from horse-drawn cars to electrically-powered vehicles didn't take place until the early 1890s.

When the transition did take place, extended trolley travel outside of Lawrence finally became possible—and was soon an enormous success. Two of the most popular destinations were Glen Forest Park in Methuen and Canobie Lake Park in Salem, New Hampshire, both of which were built by street railway companies eager to attract Sunday riders.

Just as trolleys replaced horse-drawn vehicles in the nineteenth century, buses replaced trolleys in the twentieth. By the 1930s, trolleys were no longer the primary source of public transportation in Lawrence.

Loomfixers were well-paid, highly-skilled tradesmen who worked within the textile industry maintaining, repairing, and reconditioning looms. In this 1914 photograph, a group from the local union poses in front of the widow Jacque's boarding house at 439 Essex Street, about to depart for Manchester, N.H., and a picnic at Pine Island Park.

Six

Memorable Events

Like all cities, Lawrence has had its share of celebrations, strife, and disasters. Many, like the Great Cyclone of July 26, 1890, have attracted national attention.

The tornado touched down near the Cricket Grounds, off Andover Street, just after 9 am. Suddenly, unsuspecting South Lawrence residents on Newton, Emmet, Salem, Durham, Merrimack, Springfield, and Portland Streets found themselves in a path of whirling devastation. In less than half an hour six people were dead, more than fifty were injured, and many homes—like this one on Springfield Street—were damaged or destroyed.

HARPER'S WEEKLY.
A JOURNAL OF CIVILIZATION

Vol. IV.—No. 160.]   NEW YORK, SATURDAY, JANUARY 21, 1860.   [Price Five Cents.

Entered according to Act of Congress, in the Year 1860, by Harper & Brothers, in the Clerk's office of the District Court for the Southern District of New York.

The January 10, 1860, collapse of the five-story Pemberton Mill was the city's greatest disaster. It led to changes in mill construction methods, insurance requirements, and fire inspection nationwide.

Poorly-cast iron support pillars caused the sudden afternoon collapse, burying 670 workers. As rescue teams pick-axed their way through the rubble that evening, a lantern broke, igniting a fire that quickly raged out of control. When all was said and done, 88 people were dead and 275 were injured. Abraham Lincoln was among the many who visited Lawrence in the wake of the tragedy.

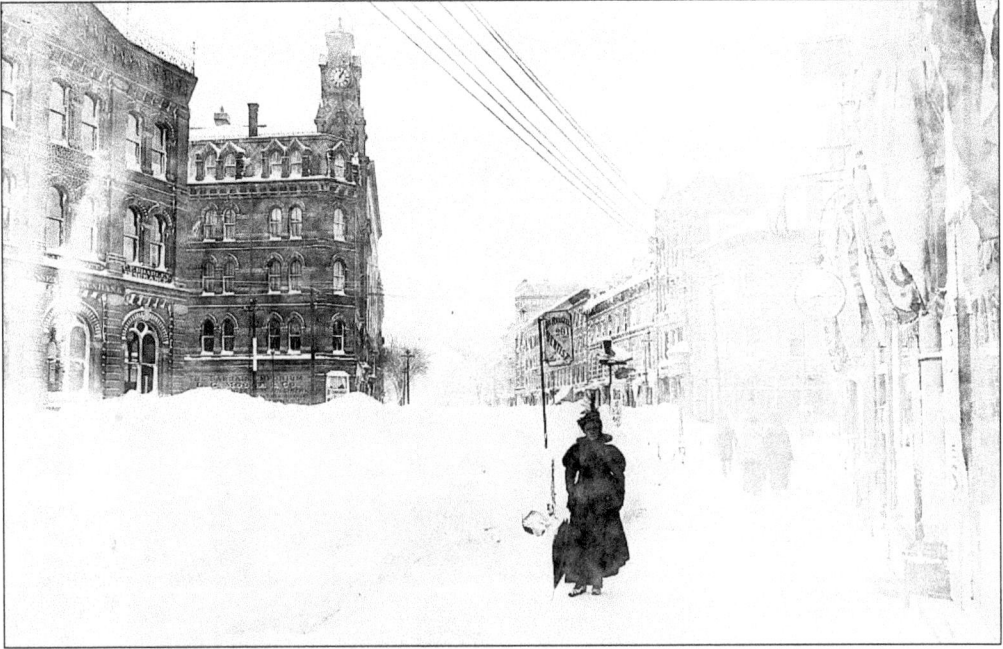

Lawrence's biggest blizzard of the nineteenth century occurred on February 1, 1898, when the city was paralyzed by 30 inches of snow blowing into drifts 8 feet deep. This photograph of Essex Street gives an excellent view not only of the drifts, but of the Odd Fellows Building as well.

Built from 1874 to 1875 on the southwest corner of Essex and Lawrence Streets, the ornately-towered structure was the new home of the city's oldest fraternal organization, the Independent Order of Odd Fellows. Once also home, at various times, to the Lawrence Public Library, the L.C. Moore Department Store, and Brockleman's Market, the building was partially destroyed by fire on Pearl Harbor Day, December 7, 1941.

One of Lawrence's most spectacular fires took place at the City Flour Mills on July 23, 1907. Located on the south bank of the Merrimack near the canal and Falls Bridge, the brick buildings contained huge amounts of corn and grain which ignited quickly—and rather suspiciously. Despite the fast response of local firefighters, the blaze raged on for nearly three days as thousands of spectators watched. When it was over, the mills were in ruins and were never rebuilt.

HARPER'S WEEKLY

A JOURNAL OF CIVILIZATION

Vol. LVI.   New York, February 10, 1912   No. 2877

The Lawrence Textile Strike of 1912 involved more than 25,000 workers and lasted for more than 10 weeks. Frustration over low wages, poor working conditions, and frequent unemployment culminated in a walkout on January 11, when textile workers discovered lower wages in their pay envelopes as the result of a new law reducing their work week by two hours.

The strike spread quickly and soon involved all the city's mills—and workers of every nationality and skill. The local branch of the International Workers of the World (IWW) requested help from their headquarters in New York. Experienced organizers were dispatched immediately and a local strike committee, representing various ethnic groups, was formed to serve as a link to strikers on matters of strategy, picketing, and relief.

92

Lawrence authorities were soon overwhelmed with the task of maintaining law and order. By January 15, Governor Foss had ordered militia companies from other parts of Massachusetts into the city to aid police. Confrontations often led to violence, resulting in the death of two strikers.

Since the strike took place in the cold of winter and food, coal, and warm clothing were in short supply, it was especially hard on the children. Many striking residents sent their young ones to sympathetic families in other communities. Transports departed from the Boston and Maine Railroad Station until police and militia stepped in on February 24 to stop the exodus. Fifteen children and their parents were taken to the police station.

The train station incident and other abuses—including a "dynamite plot" in January which was attributed to the strikers but later discovered to have been a plant by their opposition—led to a Congressional investigation of conditions in Lawrence.

On March 12, 1912, the American Woolen Company, concerned over public reaction to the hearings, agreed to the strikers' demands. By the end of the month the other mills followed. The city celebrated with a victory march—shown here approaching the intersection of Common and Lawrence Streets—and the children returned home.

Semi-centennial festivities were held June 1–3, 1903, to celebrate the 50th anniversary of Lawrence's incorporation as a city. Residents of every nationality took part in parades, regattas, team sports, bicycle, pigeon, and dog races, concerts, and more. Shown on this parade float is the special blue and white Lawrence flag officially adopted for the celebration.

In the aftermath of the Great Strike of 1912, sometimes called Bread and Roses, Lawrence strove to return to normalcy despite occasional walkouts and demonstrations. On September 29, a group of so-called anarchists and outside agitators held a march in which they carried red flags and a banner with the words: "No God; No Country."

In response, the city held a huge, patriotic Flag Parade on October 12. Popularly remembered as the God and Country Parade, it consisted of 32,000 marchers, each waving the Stars and Stripes. This group from the Packard School marched behind principal Jennie McManus. In 1962 another God and Country Parade was held in commemoration.

World War I had a great impact on the city. Sam Kaplan became the first of many Lawrence residents to be inducted; of this number, about two hundred died. Here, a local group of volunteers is posed outside the Franco-Belgian Club on Mason Street, raising funds for Belgian refugees. Local ethnic groups often collected money to aid friends and relatives back home.

The 100th anniversary of the city was held in 1953. Many celebratory events took place all over Lawrence, including this fire muster at the Hayden-Schofield Playstead, seen here in this view looking toward Saratoga Street from Lawrence Street.

On March 2, 1918, fire broke out at the city's largest furniture store, Michael J. Sullivan, Inc. Located at 218–226 Essex Street, the 35,000-square-foot establishment sold everything from custom-made cabinetry to "talking machines." Although the building, also known as the Sweeney Block, suffered extensive damage, Sullivan's recovered and remained in business at the same location for decades.

As the battles in Europe were ending in 1918, a new world menace was emerging. Within a matter of months, Spanish Influenza would kill ten times the number of people who died in World War I.

In Lawrence, one in seven families was stricken with the disease. The military was called in to assist and an emergency open-air hospital, Camp Emery, was established on Tower Hill. It was here that doctors, nurses, nuns, public health workers, and civilian volunteers labored tirelessly to treat the sometimes hundreds of new cases appearing each day. Since no immediate cure was available, patients were treated with everything from aspirin to hot peppers to strychnine, often to no avail. By the time the epidemic ended, over 500,000 Americans had died.

Mother Nature really made herself felt in Lawrence—and in much of New England—during the last half of the 1930s. Within a thirty-month period the city weathered two major disasters: the '36 Flood and the '38 Hurricane.

During the '36 Flood the Merrimack began flowing *over* the Falls Bridge (shown below). On March 20, 1936, much of the city was under water, and remained without power or telephone service for an extended period. Sanitation became a grave concern, roads into Lawrence were closed to all except emergency vehicles, and over 2,000 residents had to abandon their homes, many for several weeks. Some took up temporary residence in city schools. Rescue boats, like the one shown here at the corner of Salem and Osgood Streets, became common sights. When the waters finally receded, flood damage totaled several million dollars.

On September 21, 1938, Lawrence again felt nature's force. This time it was a hurricane. Roofing blew off the Sacred Heart and St. Laurence O'Toole Churches, the WLLH Radio antenna on top of the Cregg Building cracked and tumbled, and thirty-five huge trees on the common were destroyed.

Many national political figures have sought Lawrencians' votes over the years, sometimes almost running over each other in the process! In the fall of 1912, for example, a president and an ex-president arrived on the same day: former President (and candidate) Teddy Roosevelt in the morning, incumbent President Taft in the afternoon.

In October 1952, President Harry Truman (above center) and soon-to-be-elected Dwight D. Eisenhower (below) spoke to crowds on the common within four days of each other. Truman, who was at the end of his term, was here on October 17 to drum up votes for Adlai Stevenson for president and John F. Kennedy for senate. On October 21, Ike arrived on his own behalf, campaigning before a crowd of between 25,000 and 30,000.

Seven

A Sense of Neighborhood

Built in the early 1700s at the corner of East Haverhill and Elm Streets, the Bodwell house, razed by the city in 1957, was considered the oldest dwelling in Lawrence. The "Old Elm," so the legend goes, was planted by an Indian on July 29, 1729, the day Henry Bodwell III was born.

Today, most "old" homes in the city are two and three-deckers which once housed multiple families of textile workers, or Victorians built for owners who could afford single-family occupancy. While some of these buildings have retained their original appearance, many look different now—as do the neighborhoods surrounding them.

Lawrence neighborhoods have always had a changing face. In the city's earliest days, for example, many Irish lived in a South Lawrence shanty settlement called the Patch. The area now known as the Arlington district was once Stevens Village, built near a pond of the same name. And will the thousands who once lived in tenements in the Plains ever really get used to the way that neighborhood looks today?

Ethnic businesses, serving their respective nationalities as well as the general population, have been in Lawrence virtually since its inception. These establishments became especially prominent from the 1880s on, as each new immigrant group settled in the city. Here, in 1918, is Gaudreau's Hardware Store, located on Franklin Street in the heart of what, at the time, was a busy French-Canadian enclave. The gentlemen are, from left to right: Mr. Lamontagne, David Marquis Sr. (a house painter), and owner Louis Gaudreau.

To better understand and appreciate just how much neighborhoods change, look closely at this 1873 panorama, overlooking North Lawrence from Methuen Street to the sparsely-developed "over the Spicket" area. Virtually all the structures visible from behind the Ordway Block in the foreground to St. Mary's Church in the background have been demolished.

Many religious customs and celebrations from the "old country" were transferred to Lawrence and continue to this day. Some Roman Catholic churches, for example, still have a May Queen and a May procession, like this one at St. Mary's in 1904.

The Feast of the Three Saints, started in 1923 in Lawrence's Little Italy around Common Street, and the Lebanese Mahrajan both take place the weekend before Labor Day. In June the Portuguese still celebrate the Holy Ghost Festival, with a large procession and dinner in their own hall on Erving Street.

Jeremiah F. O'Leary, a fireman at Lawrence Engine Company No. 7 housed on Park Street, poses with his fire engine in front of the fine homes on Haverhill Street in 1896.

Most of the Irish who arrived in Lawrence early on were unskilled laborers employed to construct the Great Stone Dam, canals, mills, and other buildings necessary to create a major textile center. Within a generation, however, those possessed with ambition, perseverance, and fortitude often found success as tradesmen or merchants. The above photograph shows success in the Arlington District: William J. Kiley's Market at 298 Park Street, c. 1893.

Junk dealers who bought and sold tin, glass, paper, and rags were a familiar sight in Lawrence—and many children earned a few pennies by collecting and selling these items. Oscar Graichen, a German immigrant in 1873, was able to develop a thriving business based at 54–56 Park Street.

After the Spicket River bed was straightened in the 1880s, a bridge at Short Street provided access from the city center to this section, which would soon become a neighborhood populated by immigrants from Poland, Lithuania, and other countries. Looking northerly from the Short Street Bridge in 1897, about the only building to be seen is the Society of Friends Meeting House on Avon Street. Although the Quakers had a long history in Lawrence, today this building is home to Iglesia Cristana Methodista.

It has been estimated that at the turn of the century there were only about 600 to 800 people of Polish descent living in Lawrence. Most labored in textile mills and practiced the Roman Catholic faith. By 1905, Holy Trinity Church had been built with monies collected from these new immigrants. This photograph shows a funeral cortege at Holy Trinity, conducted by the Rosinski Funeral Home around 1922.

Saturday afternoon sports at the Spicket Playstead—now the Hayden/Schofield Playstead—on the corner of Lawrence and Myrtle Streets. Old and young came to participate and watch the games of baseball, rugby, and soccer. The teams playing were often sponsored by textile mills, ethnic clubs, or neighborhoods.

The Leopold Apron and Children's Clothing Company was a small garment factory started by German immigrants in the Back Bay neighborhood at 68 R. Woodland Street. This photograph of the seamstresses was taken c. 1920. The building was later occupied by the manufacturer of Dodge'em Bumper Cars, once found in amusement parks from coast to coast.

Born in Newburyport in 1817, John Rodman Rollins graduated from Dartmouth College and began his career as a teacher. In 1853 he became paymaster of the Essex Company and later served two terms as mayor of Lawrence. Following distinguished service in the Civil War, Captain Rollins was eventually appointed cashier of the Pacific Mills, a position he held for many years. Noted also as a historian, writer, genealogist, and long-time member of the city's school board, he died in 1892. The Rollins School on Prospect Hill was named in his memory.

Wolf's Bakery, one of many immigrant bakeshops, was located on the corner of Prospect and Ferry Streets. In addition to serving customers in the store, Wolf also used delivery wagons to service many Lawrence households.

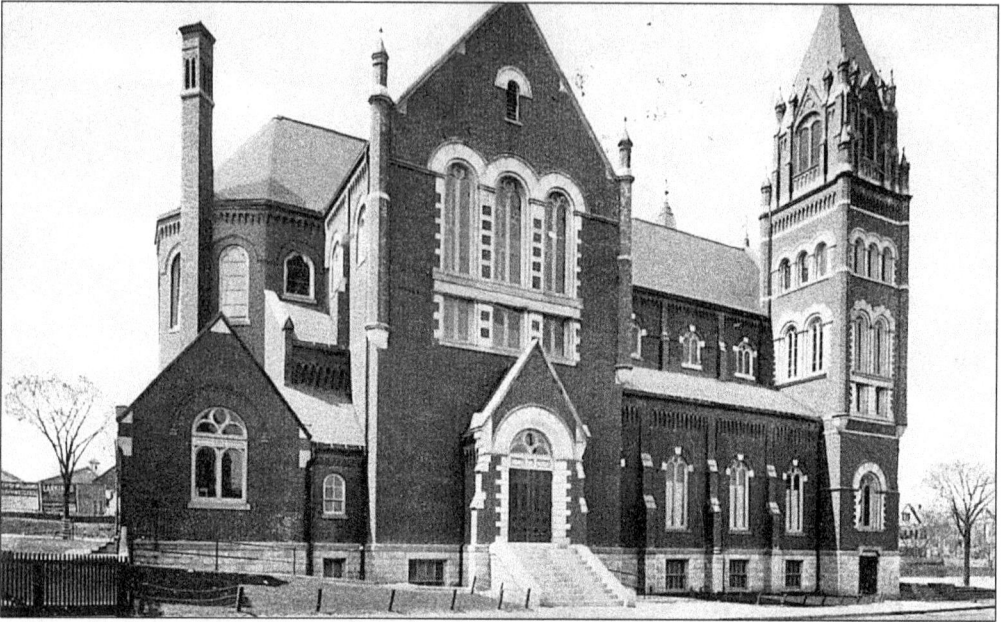

The St. Laurence O'Toole Church, demolished in 1980, was constructed 1903–08 on the triangle between East Haverhill and Newbury Streets. It was surrounded by St. Laurence's Grammar School, the Rectory, and the convent for the Sisters of Notre Dame.

Earlier, this mostly Irish parish had worshiped on the corner of Essex and Union Streets in the church now called Holy Rosary. Early Italian and Polish immigrants were allowed to celebrate Mass in the basement chapel of old St. Laurence until they were numerous and prosperous enough to support churchs of their own.

The Archdiocese in Boston, represented in Lawrence by the priests of St. Mary's, the mother church, determined when and where new mission churches for Lawrence immigrants could be established. The practice continues today.

This typical block of Lawrence tenements, with stores at street level, was owned by the Hyder brothers, Lebanese immigrants. It stood at the corner of Elm and White Streets, in the center of the Plains, a neighborhood which has always been home to many different ethnic groups.

The Lithuanian Umpa family, photographed in their vegetable garden at 185 Chestnut Street in 1905. Mr. and Mrs. I.B. Umpa and their two young sons pose proudly in their cabbage patch. The three young women are Lithuanian mill girls who boarded with the Umpa family. Many immigrant families took in boarders to supplement their income. Boarders and their hosts usually belonged to the same ethnic group.

The Philip Millman family, Jewish immigrants from Russia, owned and operated a grocery store at 269 Chestnut Street. Seen here are Philip Millman and his daughter Rebecca Zidle, c. 1916.

The Millman family was very active in Jewish community life in Lawrence. Shown here c. 1916, they entertained family and guests in their home above the store. Their kitchen looks very similar to those found in most tenements in the city.

Vincenza Casale was the only child in her family to emigrate from Italy. Shown here working in her uncle's drug store at 88 Lawrence Street around 1920, she would meet eventually meet and marry Richard Ciccarelli, a pharmacy student. Together they would live the classic immigrant success story—raising a family and operating their own business, the Lawrence Street Drug and Chemical Company.

Most of the structures here in plain view were demolished in the 1960s and '70s, as part of what became a controversial national project called urban redevelopment. Besides a significant portion of Essex Street, the tenement districts of North Lawrence—encompassing over 30 acres—were also systematically destroyed.

This c. 1953 view, looking northwesterly from the intersection of Common and Lawrence Streets, shows the intersection of Common and Amesbury Streets (at left). Today, the Buckley Garage occupies much of the parking area seen in the foreground.

A German Day Parade float on Union Street in 1910 features a banner with the inscription "Einigkeit Macht Stark" (unity makes strong), a slogan that could speak for many societies formed by immigrants in Lawrence.

Immigrants, who often arrived in Lawrence without family and friends, needed the security found in groups. The churches often provided aid, but within a few years, organizations were formed by bringing together people from the same nationality, region, or even town. Other societies were formed based on common interests. People established co-operative stores, protective societies, schools, and libraries, as well as sports and performing arts clubs.

A survey of immigrant organizations in the *Lawrence Directory* listings from 1847 to 1947 documented more than six hundred entries. This network of mutual aid served as medical, life, and unemployment insurance for many years, diminishing in popularity only after the federal government began providing social services in the 1930s.

The *Lawrence Directory* of 1922 lists twenty halls that served as centers for ethnic activities that year. The interior of one of them, the German Turnvurein Hall, is pictured here.

This scarce view shows the old South Lawrence railroad station once located off Andover Street behind the J.H. Horne & Sons Company. A portion of the Horne complex is at right and the St. Patrick's Church steeple can be seen in the background. This station handled both passengers and freight but was not as ornate as its North Lawrence counterpart.

Among the many breweries that made Lawrence famous was the Cold Spring Brewing Company, producer of once-popular Hacker's Ale. The enterprise, shown above around 1900, began operations in 1895 at 609 South Union Street near South Broadway, eventually occupying nearly 3 acres. During Prohibition, soft drinks were produced here. Although the company went out of business in the 1950s, a portion of the original plant still survives.

Another of the city's famous brewers was the Holihan Brothers company, organized in 1856. In 1912 the company built the Diamond Spring Brewery on Beacon Street, which today contains apartments.

FRANK E. CARLETON,

Contractor, Builder and Dealer in Real Estate.

☞ See Carleton's Model Houses at "Carleton-ville," Andover Street. The Most Attractive Homes Within the Confines of Lawrence. . . .

Frank E. Carleton was a major builder in South Lawrence whose name eventually became synonymous with the section he helped develop. Carletonville, as it was known in its heyday—during the latter part of the nineteenth century and the first part of the twentieth—was a rather small but distinctive neighborhood off Andover and Newton Streets, running west toward Tewksbury Street. It became one of the most elegant residential locations in the city, offering a countrified atmosphere with easy access to both railways and street cars.

Thomas E. McDonnell came to Lawrence in the early 1900s, and in time established this prominent boarding and sales stable, shown here c. 1914, at 79 Carver Street. Horse auctions were a regular Tuesday event, heavily patronized by area farmers and teamsters. McDonnell's stables were located just around the corner from another leading South Lawrence merchant, Henry C. King.

112

Henry C. King, who was also a prosperous dealer in coal and wood, operated this grocery store, shown as it appeared in the 1890s. The establishment—located opposite St. Patrick's Church, on the northeast corner of South Broadway at Salem Street—contained one of the city scales where, by law, just about everything had to be weighed before it could be bought, sold, or delivered.

Keegan's Bakery at 113 South Broadway, c. 1916, was an Irish bakery serving a neighborhood that began when Irish workers lived in shanties on Essex Company land near the dam. The owner, Mary J.E. Keegan, poses here with her young friend Almeda King.

Almeda is wearing her Sunday best: a blue serge suit with lace collar and a pink hat with black trim and flowers. The suit was self-made at the St. Clare League on Jackson Street, where Irish girls were taught homemaking skills and trained for positions in Yankee households.

113

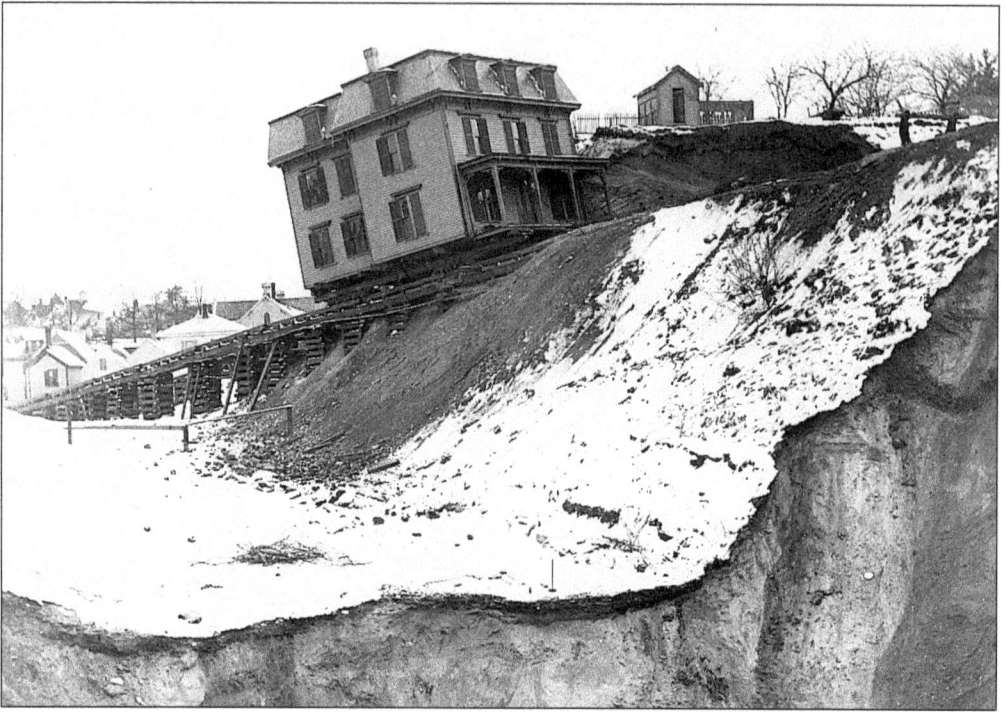

What we know today as Tower Hill was actually a group of hills. One of them, Gale's Hill—situated just above Margin Street—was named for General John Gale, who owned most of the land on the promontory.

The sandy soil on Gale's Hill was always prone to landslides, requiring makeshift bridges like the one that crossed Essex and Greenwood Streets. The continuing hazards caused the hill to be leveled in the 1890s, requiring this house to be moved to a new location at 938–940 Essex Street.

The Bruce School on Ames Street in the Tower Hill neighborhood was finished in 1902 as part of a school-building program that began in 1892. The plan also produced the Rollins School on Howard Street, the Tarbox School on Alder, the Wetherbee on Newton, the Hood on Park Street, and the Breen School on Osgood Street. All Lawrence neighborhoods now had new public schools, handsome structures, to educate the ever-growing number of immigrant children.

The first graders of the Warren Street School in 1911 reflect the ethnic mixture of the Lower Tower Hill neighborhood. Since before the Civil War, blacks had found a home in Lawrence; in fact, the first person of color to reside here was John Levy, a barber who arrived in 1846 to open a hairdressing "saloon" at 8 Turnpike Street (now called Broadway). Blacks at first worshiped in the Olive Baptist Church, then at Third Baptist, which is still located on Warren Street today.

A view of "Five Points," as seen from Bodwell Park around the turn of the century. This is where Hancock, Melrose, Melvin, Margin, and Bodwell Streets converged. The church steeple just left of center in the background belongs to St. Mary's.

This celebration of Independence Day, c. 1920, brought together members of the Hamblet, Clark, and Greene families in front of the family home at 506 Lowell Street. The house was built by Eben E. Foster about 1865, and was occupied by members of the Hamblet family until 1995.

Eight

All Work, No Play?

All was not toil in the Immigrant City. Many people remember Lawrence very differently from the way it is sometimes portrayed by historians today. For those people, it was not a gloomy factory town with nothing to offer but struggle and strife. On the contrary, Lawrence was a city of pride and excitement.

After all, where else in the country could you find not only the largest mill building in the whole world, but also a street with four movie theaters in a row, and a fifth just across the way? Nowhere, according to *Ripley's Believe It Or Not*. And how many other cities could boast the number of musicians and bands bred in Lawrence? Certainly very few.

Yes, people here worked hard and long, sometimes under conditions unfathomable today. But it is just as important to remember that they also had fun, packing a lot of activity—and even adventure—into whatever leisure time they had.

This photograph of Theater Row on Broadway shows the Astor, Modern, Broadway, and Palace Theaters. The Victoria, or State, was across the street. When this *c.* 1949 photograph was taken, four additional movie theaters—the Capitol, Premier, Star, and Warner—were also providing entertainment in Lawrence.

Of all the parks in Lawrence none is larger, and perhaps more controversial, than Den Rock. Initially planned by the city to be a cemetery, superstitions surrounding its origins and "mysterious happenings" were once commonplace, and continued right into the twentieth century.

This c. 1900 photograph is of the rock for which the park was named. At the time this picture was taken, Den Rock Park was one of the most popular recreational areas in Lawrence, encompassing some 80 acres.

Glen Forest was also a popular recreational area. Technically located in Methuen, it usually advertised itself as being in Lawrence, for it sat just below Tower Hill, sloping toward the river. Its 43 wooded acres were maintained by the Lawrence and Lowell Division of the Boston & Northern Street Railway Company, who built the park as a way to attract Sunday riders to its trolleys.

The theater at left featured some of the finest vaudeville acts in New England, and the bandstand to its right regularly offered musical concerts. Dancing, boating, and bowling were also available, and admission to the park was free.

In 1888, the three-year-old Lawrence Canoe Club, needing to expand, moved from McFarlin Court on the north side of the river, to Shattuck Street on the south. This new boathouse, designed by George G. Adams, was built on land supplied by the Essex Company. Besides boating and canoe racing, the club also offered bowling and tennis, and even supported a baseball team for a while.

Before long, the Canoe Club's popularity had residents from surrounding communities competing feverishly for membership. Methuen millionaire Henry C. Nevins, for example, served as vice-commodore for a time. The club declined in the 1940s and the Lawrence Experiment Station stands on the site today.

A turn-of-the-century view of the *Startled Fawn*, one of many popular excursion boats that traveled the Merrimack, both above and below the Great Stone Dam. Especially busy on weekends, some of these vessels could carry over a hundred passengers.

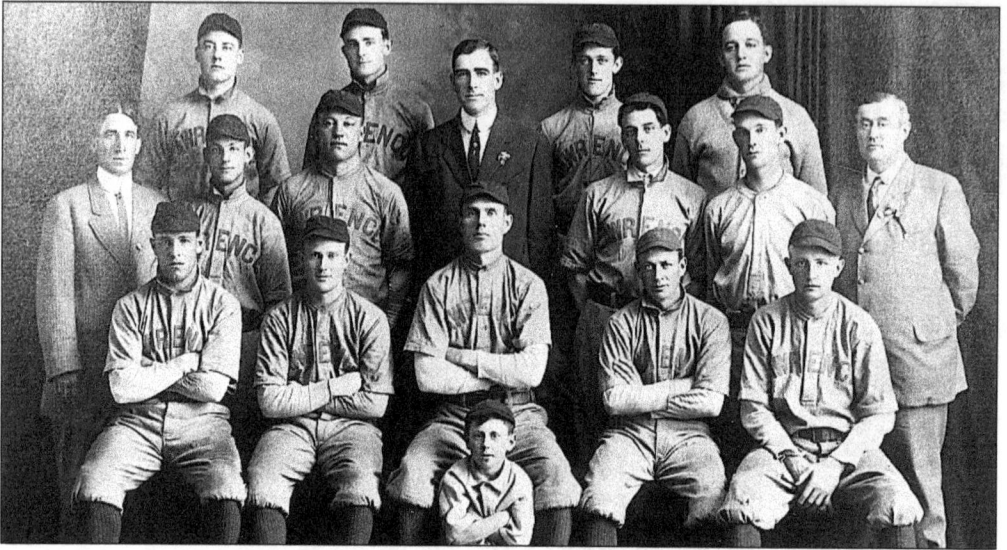

Semi-professional baseball was once enormously popular here and throughout New England, especially when teams from different cities played each other.

The Lawrence Baseball Club is shown here in 1912, the year they were champions of the New England League. Although African-Americans weren't accepted into the majors until Jackie Robinson started for the Brooklyn Dodgers in 1947, they were obviously an important part of Lawrence's winning teams.

Most semi-professional clubs played at O'Sullivan Park on Water Street, where the Boy's Club is located today. In 1924 famous athlete Jim Thorpe played baseball there, with the Lawrence Independents.

Mullaney Park on Bodwell Street, known back in 1900 as The Amphitheatre, was one of five parks, besides the common, given to Lawrence by the Essex Company. In 1912 the number of city parks began growing substantially as Lawrence established a system of supervised playgrounds.

Until 1913, the city provided for swimming by maintaining a number of municipal bathhouses on the Merrimack. When a runway to one of them collapsed that summer, killing eleven young boys, the bathhouses were abolished. Nine years later the first municipal swimming pool was built, behind the jail off Hampshire Street. By 1924 the city had 185 acres of parks and playsteads.

Mark H. Devlin taught and coached at Lawrence High School for over forty years, overseeing numerous championship teams in baseball, basketball, and football. During the 1930s he coached three undefeated football teams, two of which became state champions.

Devlin—known as "Devy" or "The Grey Fox" to colleagues and the press—was born in Lawrence in 1894. He went on to play and coach college sports and play professional football before returning home to work at Lawrence High.

This drawing, celebrating the 1945 football team, originally appeared in the *Boston Herald* and was later reprinted as a promotional handout by Kennedy's Under-Grad Shop.

Basketball, as an organized sport in America, was barely fifteen years old when this championship Lawrence High team was photographed in 1907. (And yes, those *were* their uniforms!)

Because society, for many years, regarded women's team sports as unfeminine, girls were often discouraged from participating. We have little published data today on the involvement of women in amateur sports back then.

Music was studied, played, and danced to with great enthusiasm in Lawrence. From the 1920s through the 1940s, big band music was all the rage. Lawrence musicians often began in bands made up of family or friends from the same ethnic background, playing for dances at churches and social clubs. For example, the Sears Orchestra—seen above in 1924—was an important part of Portuguese-American social life in Lawrence.

PHIL BOGRAD
TRUMPET
SAX
"CROONER"

DON TEPPER
DRUMS
XYLOPHONE

ANTHONY BARONE
PIANO
PIANO ACCORDION
TRUMPET

BILL SIMEONE
BANJO
GUITAR

AL SPITZ
BASS VIOLIN
SOUSAPHONE

FRED BOUCHER
TRUMPET
FRENCH HORN

BEN GRESKA
TROMBONE
VIOLIN

"VAL" JEAN
SAXS
CLARINET

JOS. BARBIERI
BASS
CLARINET
TRUMPET

JOHN FREDERICKSON
SAXS
CLARINET

Later, as orchestras grew and became more professional, the names of their members reflected a wider mix of nationalities. Many Lawrence musicians, some of whom are pictured here, went on to travel New England—and even the world—as sidemen or featured players in big-name bands. And while it's impossible to know exactly how many couples first met under the glitter balls of area dance halls, it's a sure bet that many did.

122

Originated and owned by the *Lawrence Eagle* and *Evening Tribune* newspapers, Radio Station WLAW broadcast from the second floor of 278 Essex Street. The station offered a good variety of syndicated programming and also gave local people the chance to do their own shows.

On Sunday mornings from 8:15 to 8:30 am, the Lawrence Christian Endeavor Union Choir performed live. Seen here in 1942, they are, from left to right: (front row) Winnie Ross, Frieda Todd, Martha Henning, Margaret Stone, Bob Kesler, Ruth Henning (organist), Fred Butterworth (song leader), and Ray Todd (at the microphone); (back row) Bill Wood, Ruth Todd, Joe Barton, Ruth Dallon, and Francis Prescott.

Church groups and religious associations were, for many years, a central part of life in Lawrence. Members not only got together to do good works, but also to socialize and have fun, often sharing parties, local outings, and stays at summer camps. The Christian Endeavor Union, a large Protestant group for teenagers and young adults in Greater Lawrence, put on this lavish production of *H.M.S. Pinafore* in 1942.

Lawrence, Mass.

Few people looking at the remaining portions of this building today would ever imagine that Chaplin once played here in person, as did Lillian Russell and a legion of comedians, magicians, singers, dancers, orchestras, and stock companies from around the world.

Built by the Sweeney brothers of Lawrence, the Colonial opened in 1904 as a showcase for the best in professional talent. Situated on the northwest corner of Hampshire and Methuen Streets, its five stories contained stores in the front portion of the first floor and a rooming house above. The immense stage section occupied the rear.

Some remember when the Hofbrau, one of the most popular entertainment spots in the city, was located here. Others—including police—will recall the strippers who wore little more than makeup and a smile when, in the 1970s, this was the infamous Chez When.

It's doubtful that any of Lawrence's social "landmarks" ever acquired a more unforgettable or intriguing nickname than did Riverside Gardens (at left) on Bay State Road. Shown here around 1940, the "Bucket of Blood" was a combination skating rink and wrestling arena.

The large building to its right was the headquarters of Jersey Ice Cream, a Lawrence business started about 1904. Sealtest eventually took it over, producing its products here until the early 1960s.

Friends Arthur Flynn and Andy Callahan are remembered as two of the city's best and most respected fighters. Each was a draw unto himself.

Flynn, who died in 1985, boxed with such greats as Gene Tunney and Jack Sharkey. In Buenos Aires in 1926, at the age of eighteen, he won a Pan American Boxing Championship. Later, he also became an accomplished wrestler, writer, and on-air personality at Radio Station WLAW.

Andy Callahan, a Prospect Hill boy, began boxing at age fourteen, while still a student at the Rollins School. He eventually went on to hold three New England Championships simultaneously, a rare accomplishment then—and now. "The Toy Bulldog," as he liked to be called, died tragically at the Battle of Monte Cassino in World War II. He was thirty-three.

While some people may know that Lawrence once had a number of bicycle clubs, few are aware that motorcycle clubs were also popular here. Riding motorcycles for pleasure and sport is not unique to our own time; organized associations began in the U.S. as early as 1903.

This photograph of the Kimball Motorcycle Club, c. 1926, was taken in front of D.A. Kimball's bicycle and motorcycle shop at 99 Lawrence Street.

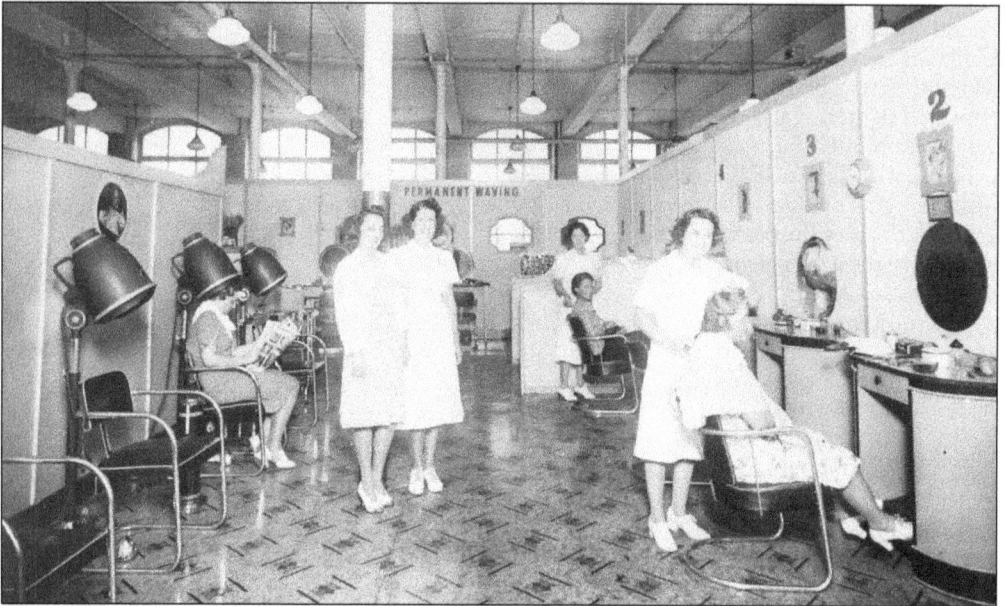

The year is 1938 and you're looking inside Tony's Hairdressing Salon, one of many businesses located in the Super Store building on Lawrence Street. That's twenty-year-old Hilda Gagne giving her friend Delia Condon a shampoo and finger wave at booth #2. (At 50¢, it was definitely cheaper than an 'updo' or a $3 perm.) Hilda, a graduate of the Lawrence Academy of Beauty Culture on Common Street, worked an average of fifty hours a week for her salary of $16.50.

Lawrencians liked their libations; there were two hundred saloons listed in the *Lawrence Directory* in 1882. One of them, John Moolic's, sat on 9 Common Street, choice property owned by the Moolic family. As was common practice at the time, the Moolic's lived upstairs over their business. That way, family members could run the bar during the day, while men took care of customers at night.

In the twentieth century, two of Lawrence's more "noteworthy" drinking establishments were The Brass Rail at 179 Valley, and Pinky's Cafe across the street at 57 Franklin. In the above photograph, some of Pinky's employees are shown in 1949. From left to right are: (front row) Celina Smerdon, Lucille LeBrasseur, Florence Murphy, Eva Sargent, and Joe LeBrasseur; (back row) Leo Topping, Shyer Rosenberg, Dave Rosenberg, Pinky Rosenberg, and Leslie Walker. The photograph below is an exterior view of the area before urban redevelopment.

Acknowledgments

A special debt of gratitude is reserved for Helen Sapuppo, Elizabeth McAuliffe, and Mary and Doug Seed for their time, patience, and invaluable assistance on this project.

We would also like to thank the following individuals, organizations, and businesses—past and present—who have assisted us in gathering information and photographs essential to the compilation of this book:

Alphabet Book and Antiques, Andover Books and Prints, Andover Historical Society, Michael J. Arakelian, M.D., Arlington Trust Company, Mary Armitage, Marilyn Bardetti, Ella Barnet, Marie Barry, Yadira Betances, Bider's Antiques, Carroll Bradish, Barbara Brown, David Burke, Genevieve E. Byrne, Thomas F. Caffrey, Esq., John H. Campbell, Rita M. Caron, Richard F. Ciccarelli, M.D., James B. Coffey, Michael Coleman, Marilyn Kaatz Cook, Cross Coal Company, Catherine Catalano DeBurro, Theresa DePippo, Tom DiGenti, James P. Dowd, James Duffen, *Eagle Tribune*, Henry C. Elwell, Dorothy Emmert, Yildiray Erdener, Ph.D., Essex Company, Rita Falco, John Faro, Barry Flynn, Genevieve Killeen Foley, Daniel W. Gagnon, Grace Episcopal Church, E. Thomas Greene, Stanley Greenwood Jr., James Gulla, Richard Hale, Marion Hall, Hamblet family, Ruth Henning, Peter Hewitt, Edward Hoegen, Hilda Gagne Holt, International Institute, Irene Karabashian, Pat Karl, E. Evelyn Kellett, Robert T. Kelley, Almeda King, Alfred Koch, Nicholas Koren, L A. Labrie, Jack Lahey, Harold Landry, Nancy Hall Laughlin, Robert E. Lautzenheiser, Lawrence Experiment Station, Harry Lehnert Jr., Marie Leone, Donald Look, John McAvoy, Robert Paul McCaffery, Ph.D., Justine Devlin McComiskey, Gertrude E. McDonnell, Mrs. Peter McKinnis, Ernest Mack, David Meehan, Shirley Meinelt, Eileen Mele, Karen A. Mello, M.D., Methuen Historical Commission, Cecile Bergeron Micka, Larry Moolic, Paula Paolino, Doris W. Parthum, Bruno A. Pietuchoff, Oscar Porst, M. Eleanor Porter, Marguerite Riley, Shyer Rosenberg, Janina Rosinski, William Schwartz, Mitzi Sciandra, Angelo Sciuto, John Sears, Ralph J. Shalhoub, Rita Shine, Amelia Stundza, Bernard Sullivan, James Sullivan, Roger Trahan Sr., Theresa Veilleux, Venerini Sisters, Ilona Korziuk Volungus, Bradford B. Wakeman, Joan and Leon Wilde, Mina Wilder, Pamela Yameen, YWCA, and Rebecca M. Zidle.

This book is dedicated to all of the members and friends of Immigrant City Archives.

Visit us at
arcadiapublishing.com

www.ingramcontent.com/pod-product-compliance
Lightning Source LLC
Chambersburg PA
CBHW080900100426
42812CB00007B/2098